SPRING 2018

IN THIS ISSUE:

AERIAL PHOTOGRAPHY IN HUDSON VALLEY
P.2

VILLA 9W: LET THERE BE WHITE
P.6

PHOTO STORY: MODERN RUSTIC
P.28

STYLE IMPROVEMENT
P.34

DINO ALEXANDER: SELLING REAL ESTATE IN STYLE
P.38

HAVING YOUR HOME PROFESSIONALLY PHOTOGRAPHED?
P.42

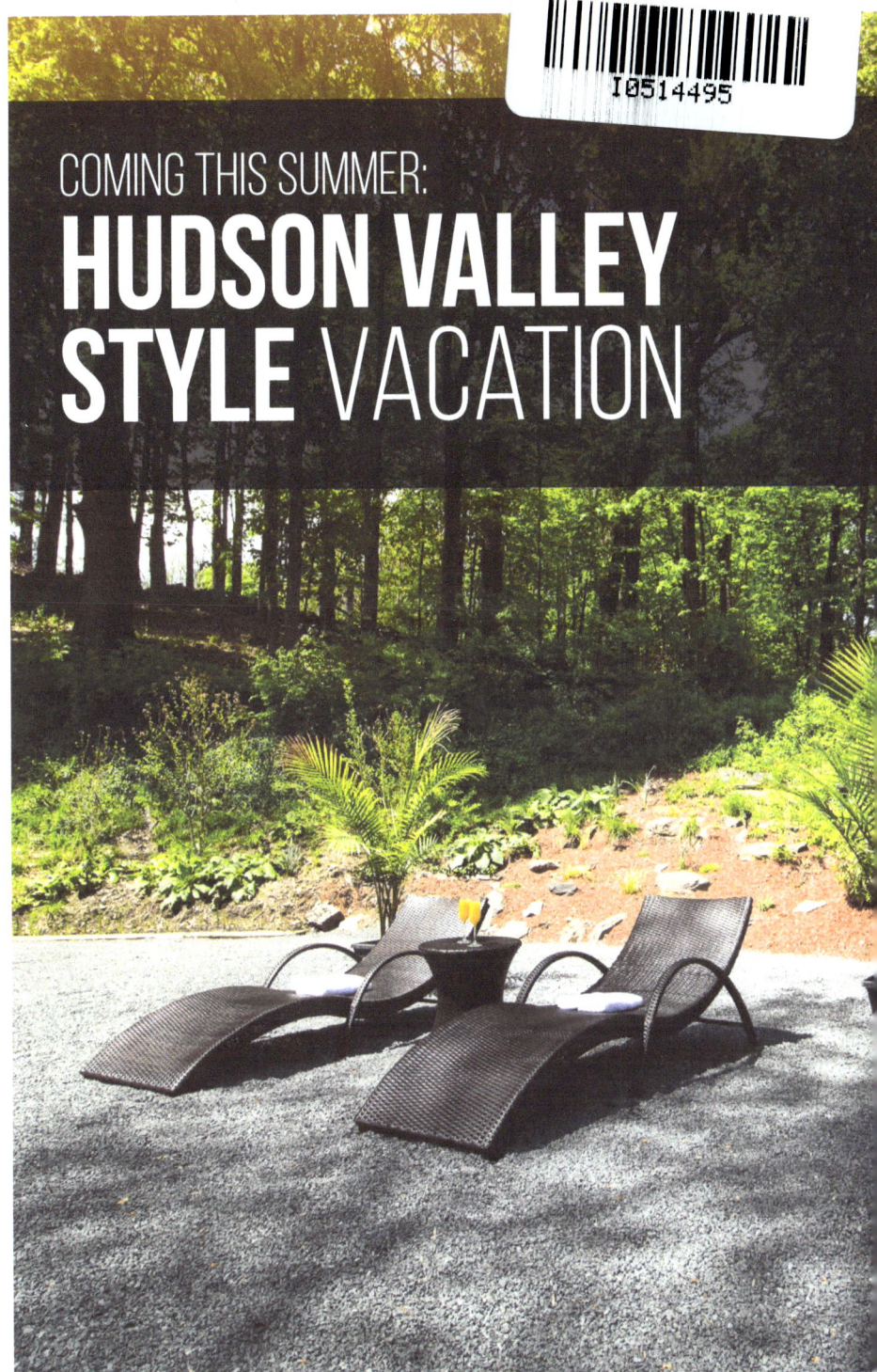

COMING THIS SUMMER:
HUDSON VALLEY STYLE VACATION

FROM THE EDITORS:

Spring is finally here! **Time to wake up and get it done!** We are trying to spend as much time outdoors as possible, before the Summer heat waves are here. Spring in Hudson Valley is magical and it's a perfect time for the Hudson Valley Style to shine through even brighter!

Maxwell Alexander & Dino Alexander

© 2018 Hudson Valley Style Magazine
A Duncan Avenue Group Publication

Contact Us:
1-845-372-5777
editors@HudsonValleyStyleMagazine.com
advertise@HudsonValleyStyleMagazine.com
info@HudsonValleyStyleMagazine.com
careers@HudsonValleyStyleMagazine.com

HUDSON VALLEY **STYLE** 1

AERIAL PHOTOGRAPHY IN HUDSON VALLEY

by Maxwell Alexander

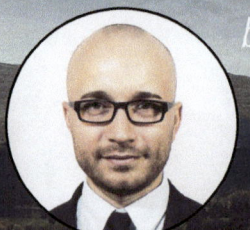

Hudson Valley Homes and Estates really do have a lot of character, not to mention that the architecture, landscaping and nature setting is truly stunning. With the backdrop of the Hudson Valley, it is a prime location for aerial drone photography. With years of experience, it is safe to say that we work diligently to make sure that our clients get the result they want out of their aerial photography and this is especially the case if they are trying to sell or market their property. With breath-taking photographs and a friendly team who will work closely with you every single step of the way, you know that you can count on us to go that extra mile while also delivering remarkable and stylish photos that you never thought possible.

HARNESSING THE POWER & BEAUTY OF NATURE

We know that nature is truly a force to be reckoned with, but in the right situation, it can also provide you with the perfect setting for an inspiring photo shoot. It doesn't matter whether it is sunset, sunrise, in the middle of a heatwave or snowing like it's Christmas Day because we have the ability to use every situation to your advantage. This means that we capture photographs like you have never seen before and it also means that the end result won't be like every other real estate photography out there.

OUR TALENTED AND FRIENDLY TEAM

Led by Maxwell Alexander, World-Class Art Director and Photographer, our team knows exactly how to approach a luxury property with flawless execution. We take into account the style of the home, the surrounding greenery and more, before planning our angle of approach and camera view. This gives us the chance to capture your home in the best possible way while also giving us the chance to provide every single viewer (your potential buyer) with a unique and magical experience.

OUR DRONES AND PILOTS

When you come to us for all of your drone photography needs and requirements, you'll find that we have the latest professional equipment and only FAA-licensed drone pilots. Not only does this mean that we are able to deliver a better result than our competitors, but it also means that we have the experience you need to really stand out from the crowd.

OUR SPECTACULAR AERIAL REAL ESTATE PHOTOGRAPHY

Aerial Photography is one of the best ways to highlight your Real Estate Property including indoor and outdoor photo and video shots. We can cover landscape features and look and feel of the neighborhood, all of it is important to your potential buyers.

If you are interested in our team, how we can help you or even to see if there is anything that we can do for you then please do get in touch with us today. We would love to hear from you and we are very excited to work with you to get you the best result out of your aerial photography.

Review Our Aerial Photography Portfolio and Schedule Your Aerial Photo Shoot at DuncanAvenue.com

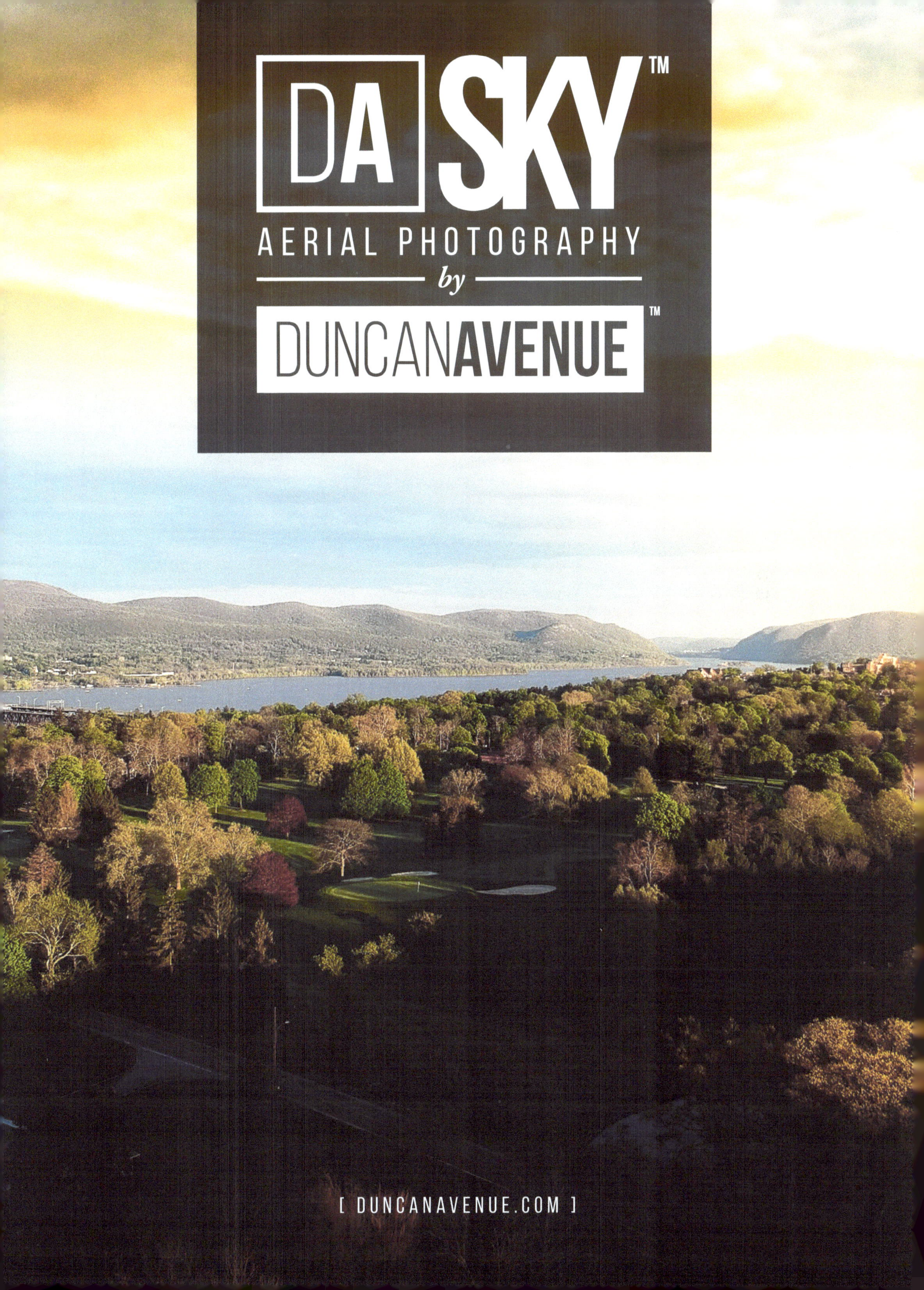

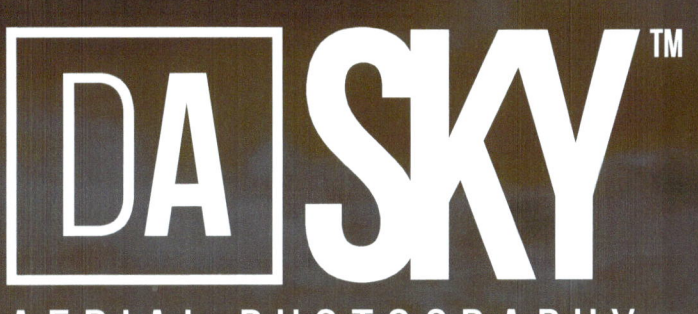

DA SKY™
AERIAL PHOTOGRAPHY
by
DUNCAN AVENUE™

[DUNCANAVENUE.COM]

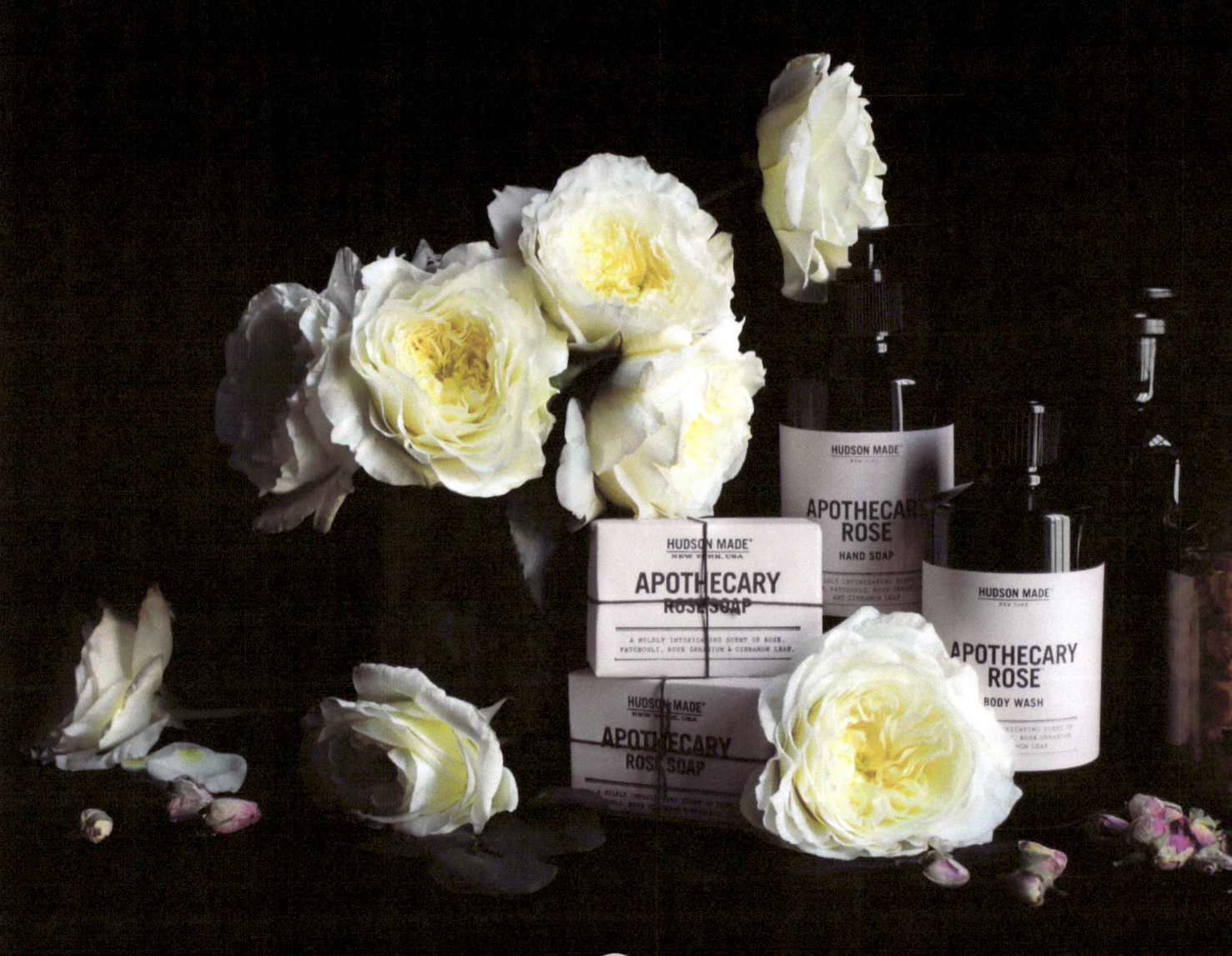

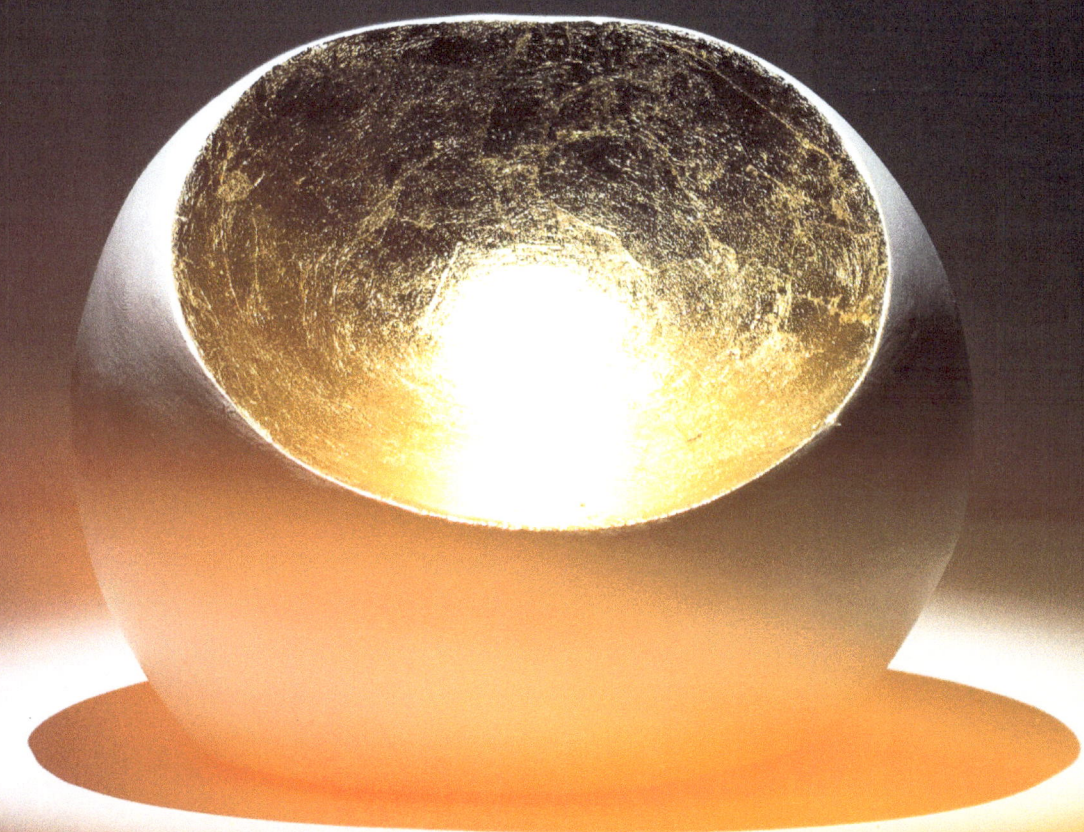

MAXWELL ALEXANDER |DESIGN™
maxwellalexander.design/sculpture

[HUDSON VALLEY STYLE LIVING]

[LET THERE BE... WHITE

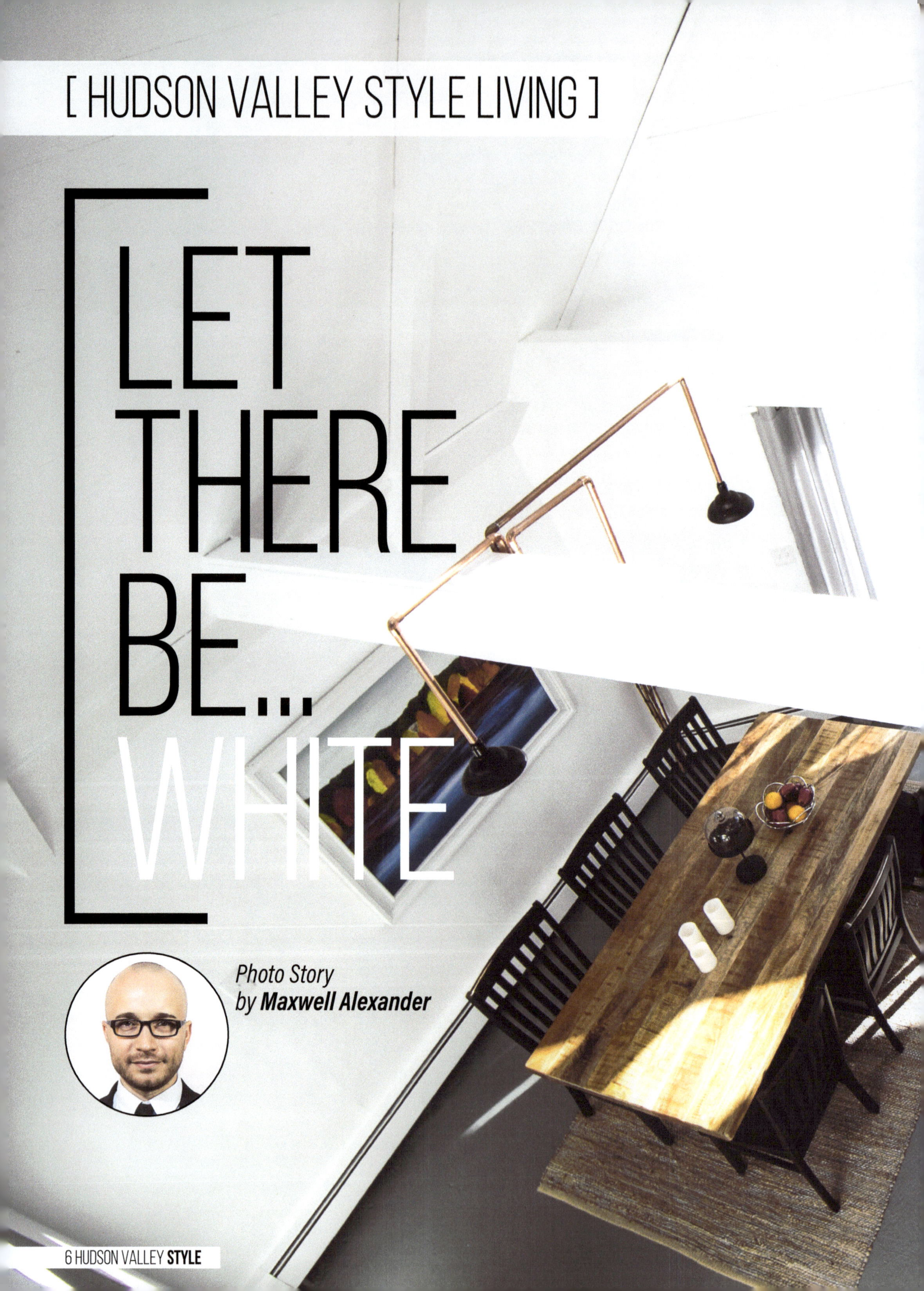

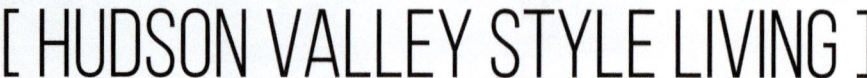

Photo Story by **Maxwell Alexander**

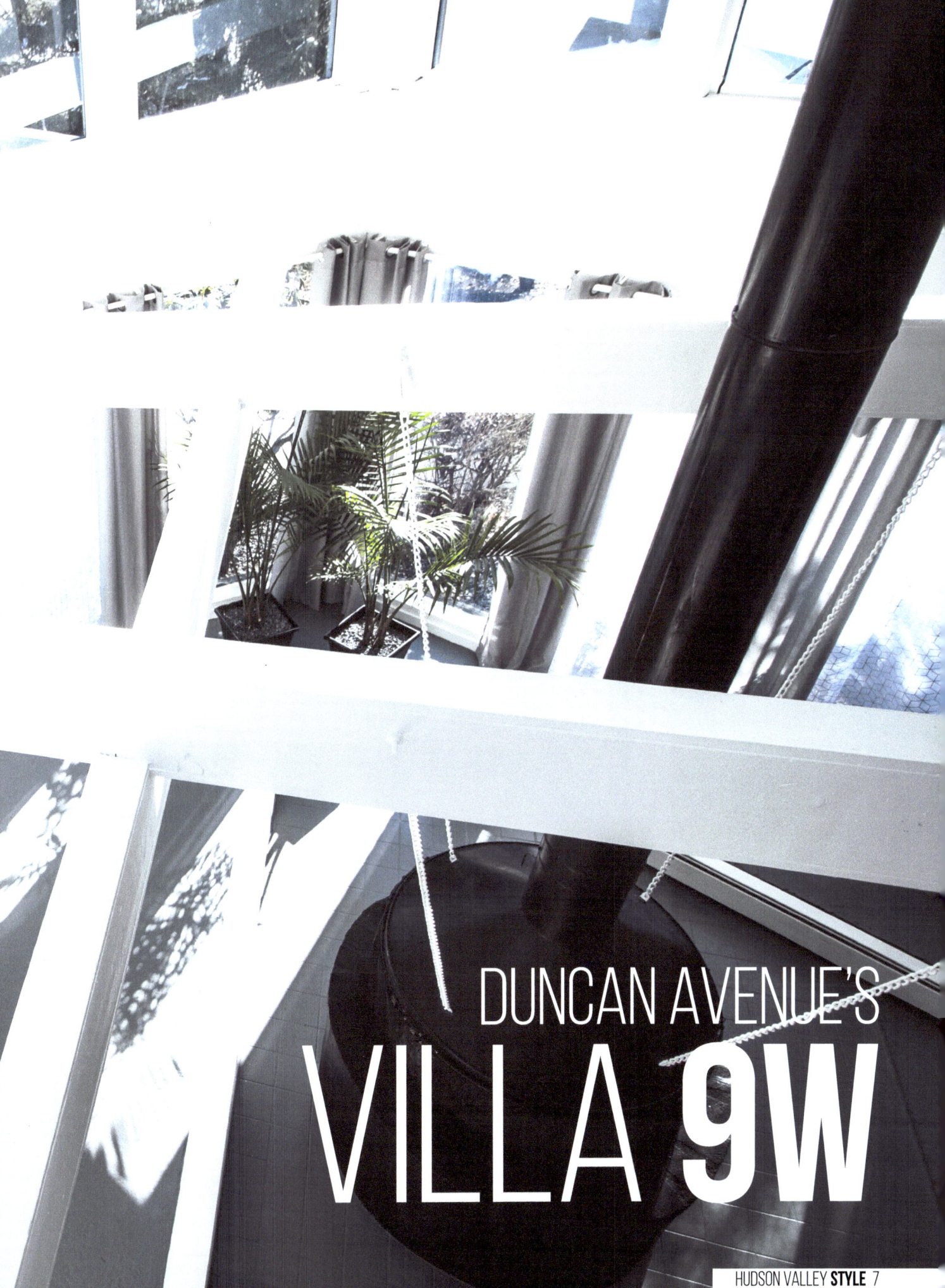

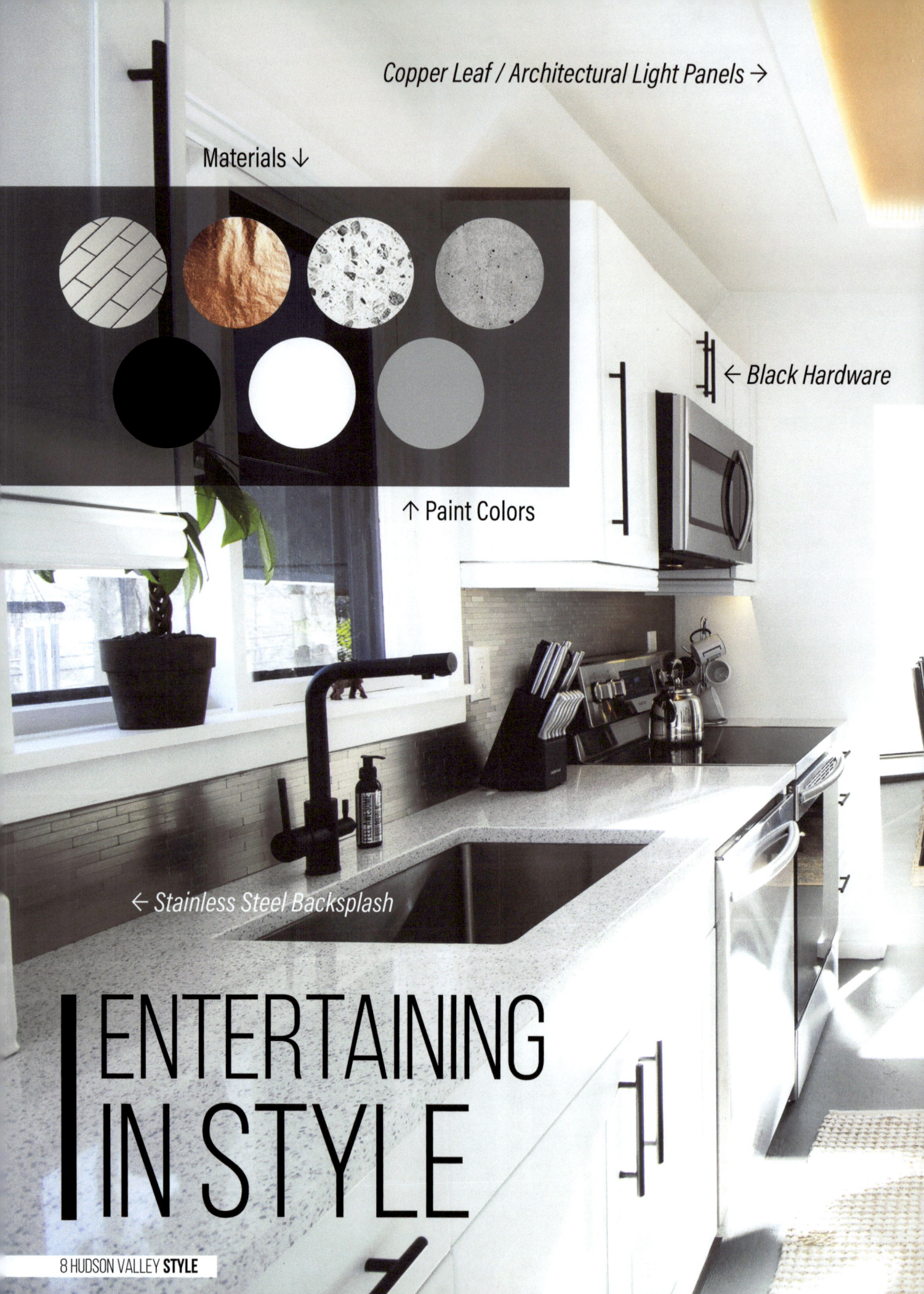

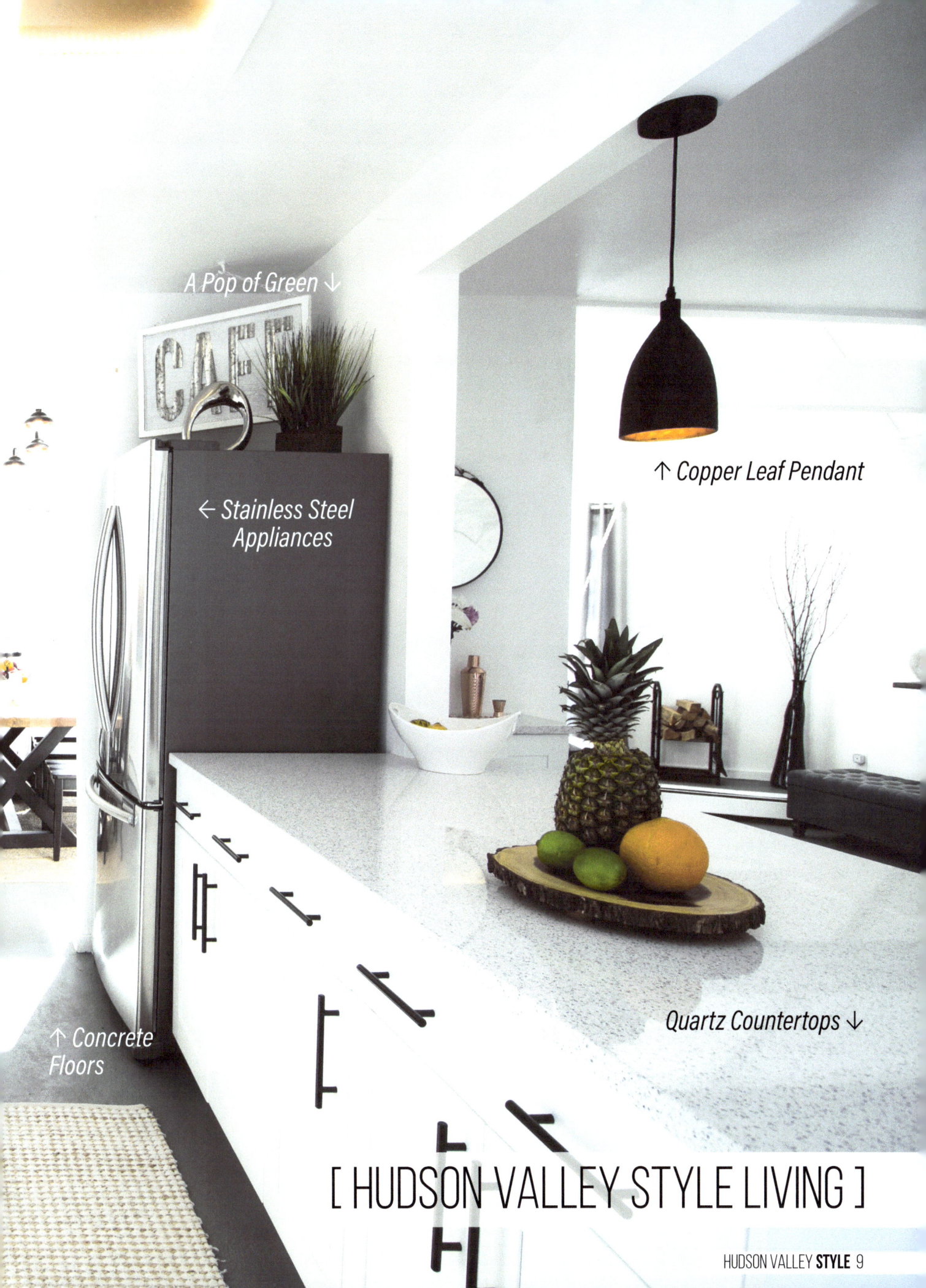

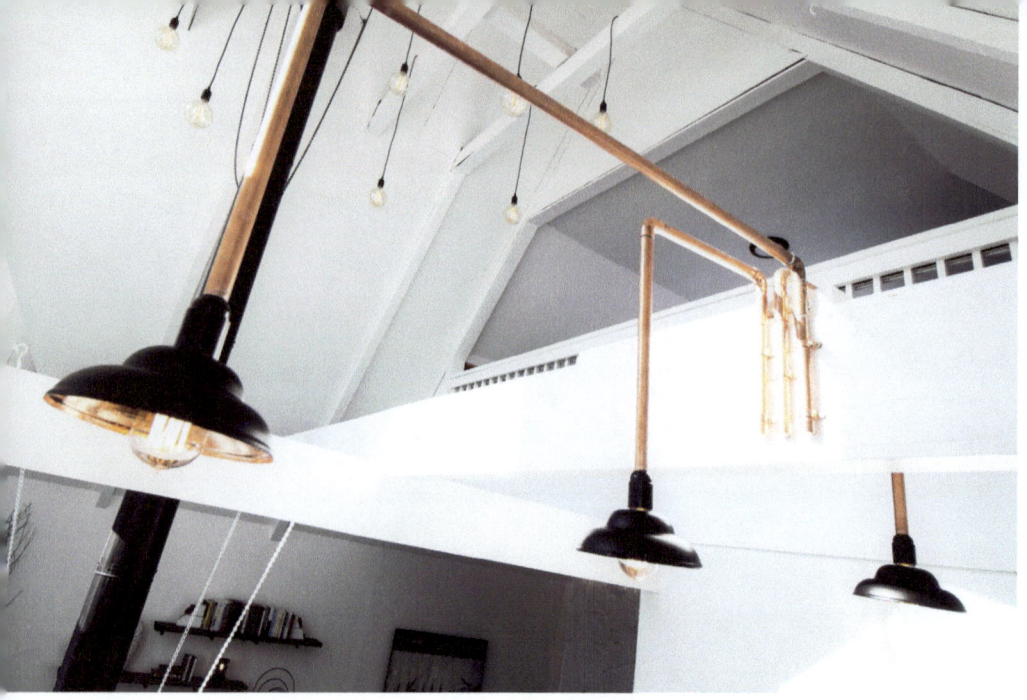

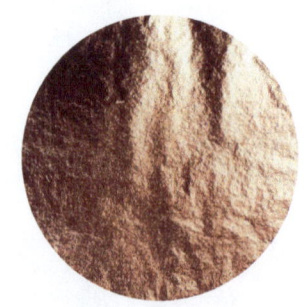

← *Custom Copper Lights*
© Duncan Avenue Design

White Granite Wall →

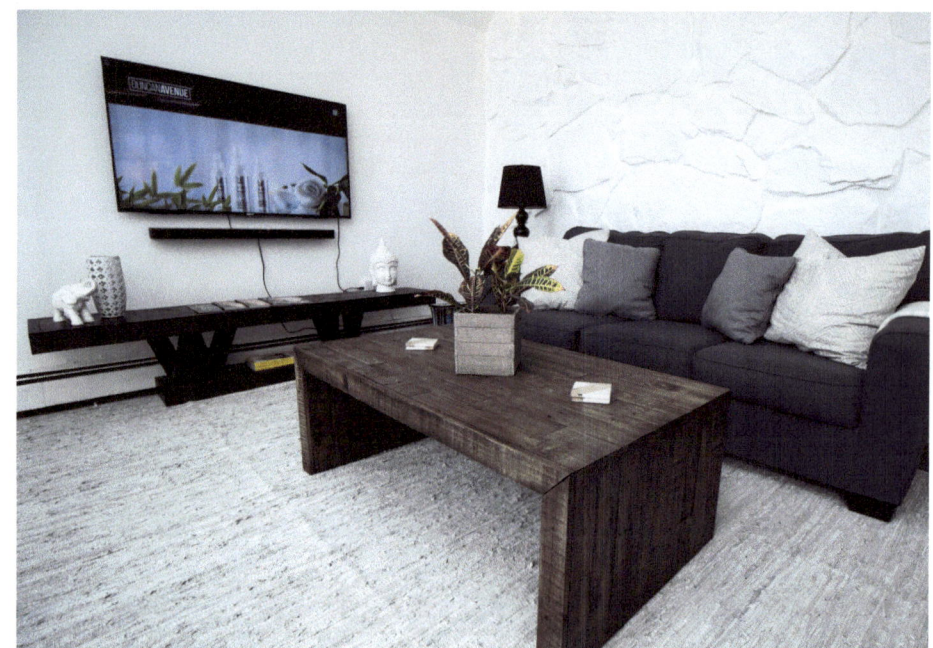

Wood Accents →

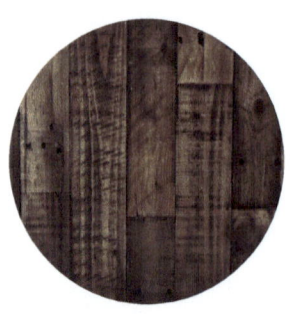

← *Formal Dining Area*

LIVING | WHITE
SPACE | BALANCE

Custom Entertainment
↓ *Console*

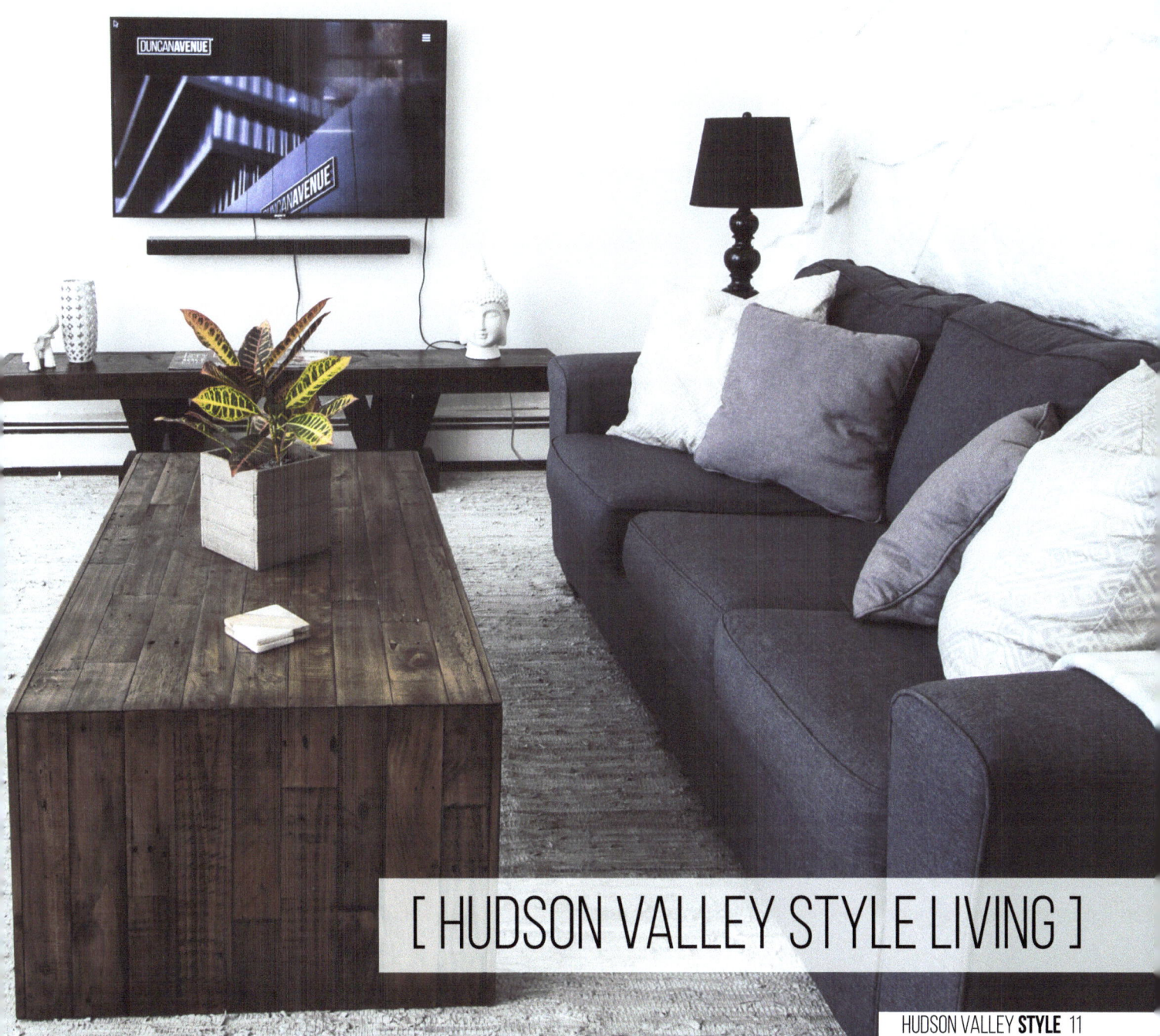

[HUDSON VALLEY STYLE LIVING]

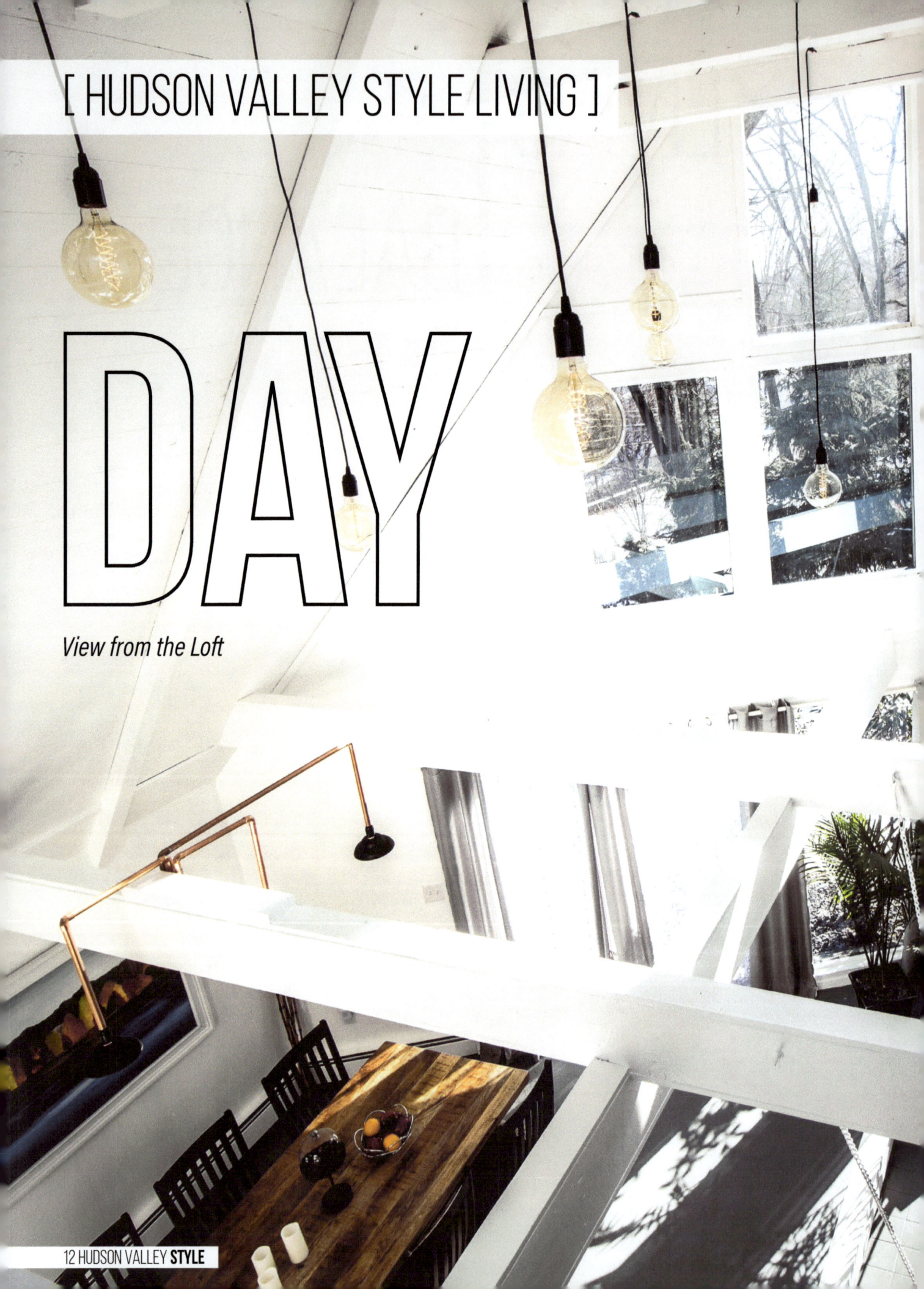

[HUDSON VALLEY STYLE LIVING]

DAY

View from the Loft

← 10 x 5" Edison Bulbs

VS
WARM

Custom Light Fixture
© Duncan Avenue Design

HUDSON VALLEY **STYLE** 13

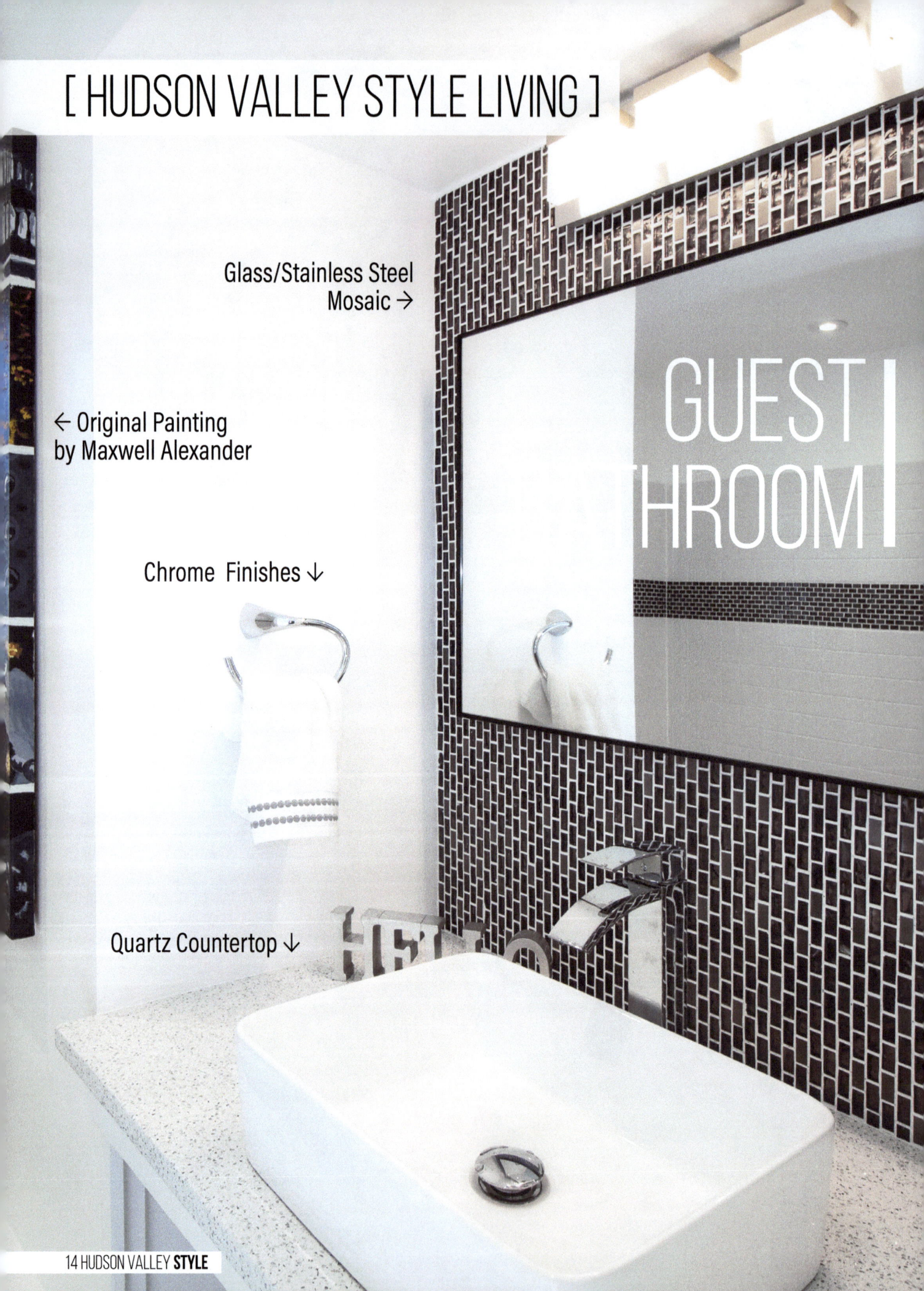

[HUDSON VALLEY STYLE LIVING]

Glass/Stainless Steel Mosaic →

← Original Painting by Maxwell Alexander

Chrome Finishes ↓

Quartz Countertop ↓

GUEST BATHROOM

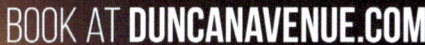

BOOK AT DUNCANAVENUE.COM

EXPERIENCE THE MAGIC OF HUDSON VALLEY FOR YOURSELF.
STAY WITH US!

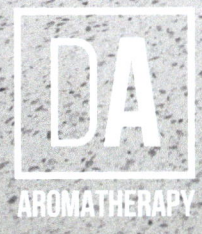
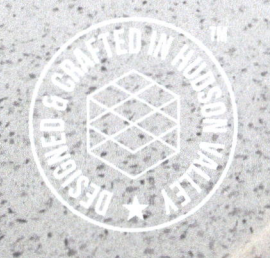

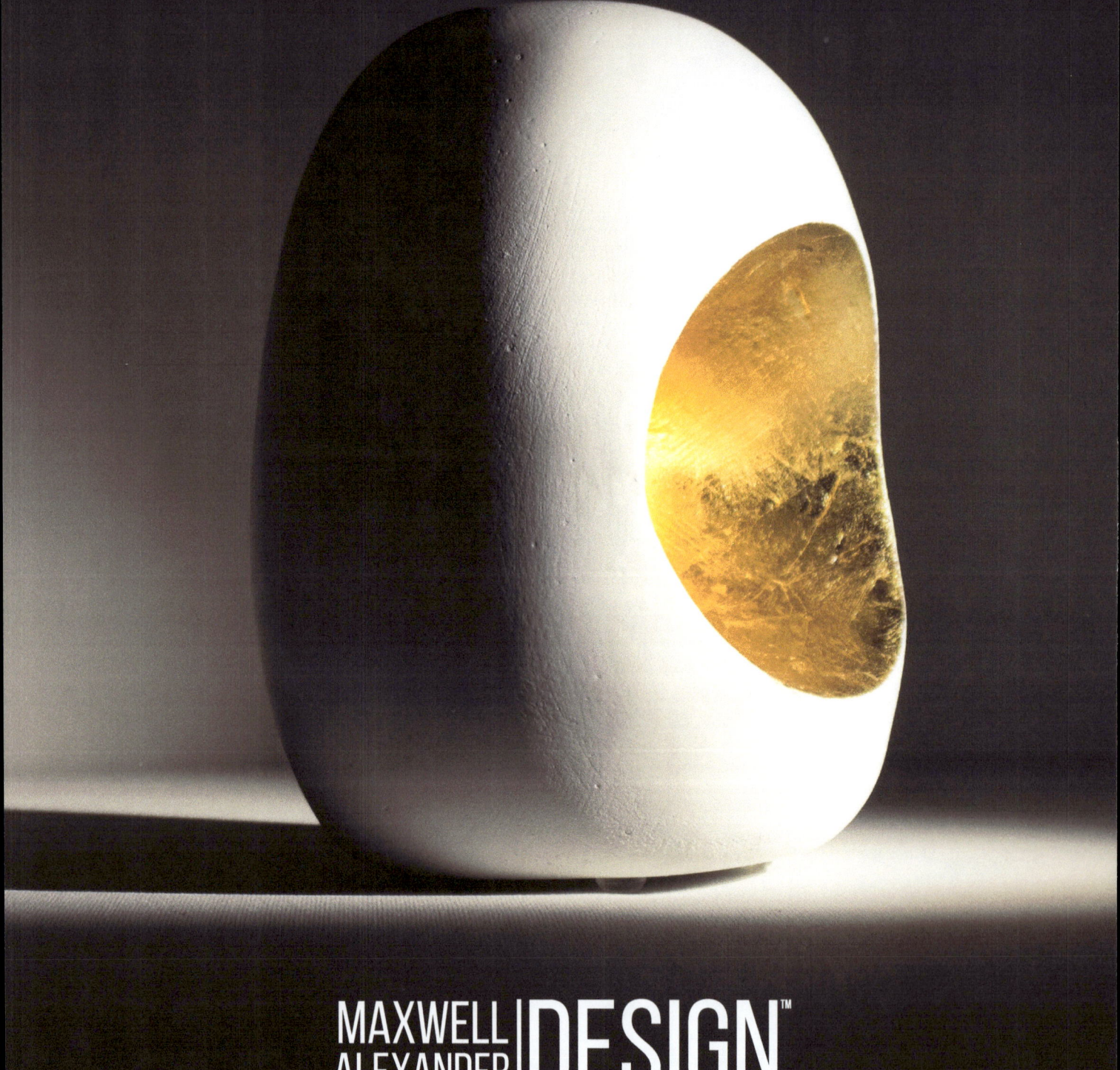

EXPERIENCE THE MAGIC OF HUDSON VALLEY™

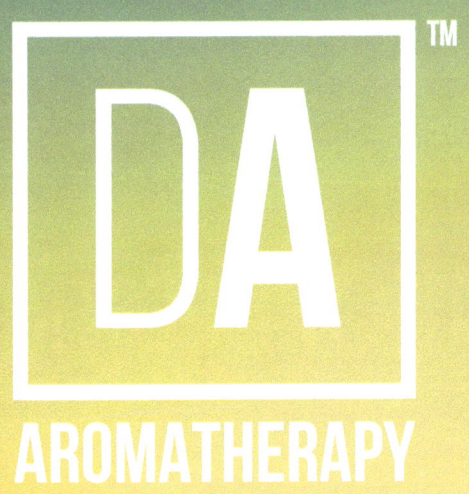

[PLANT DERIVED INGREDIENTS / NO PARABENS
NO SULFATES / NO DEA/MEA VOC-FREE / BIODEGRADABLE
CRUELTY-FREE / GOOD FOR YOU & GOOD FOR
THE ENVIRONMENT / MADE IN THE USA / DESIGNED &
CRAFTED IN HUDSON VALLEY]

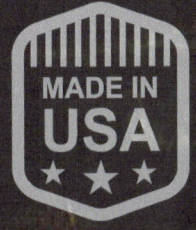 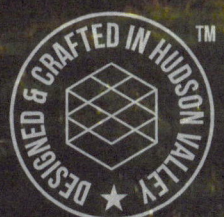 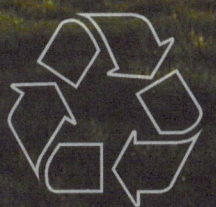 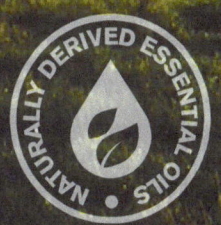 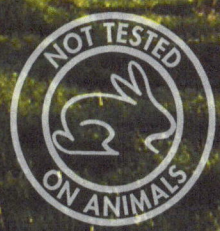

DA-AROMATHERAPY.COM

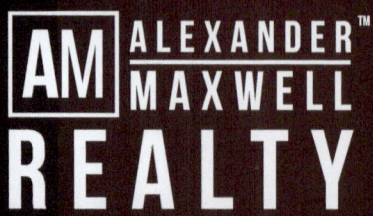

ALEXANDER MAXWELL REALTY

Luxury Hudson Valley Homes & Estates

LIST WITH THE BEST!

THE FIRST & ONLY HUDSON VALLEY REALTY THAT PROVIDES COMPLEMENTARY MARKETING SERVICES FOR EVERY LISTING:

+ PROFESSIONAL PHOTOGRAPHY
+ AERIAL/DRONE IMAGING
+ DIGITAL STAGING
+ STAGING CONSULTATION
+ FEATURE IN THE HUDSON VALLEY STYLE MAGAZINE

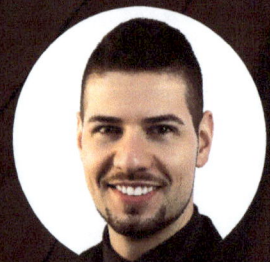

DINO ALEXANDER
PRINCIPAL BROKER

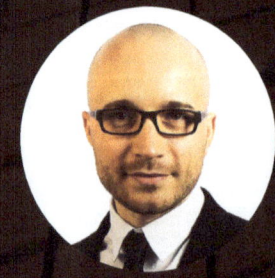

MAXWELL ALEXANDER
MARKETING & DESIGN DIRECTOR

ALMAXREALTY.COM // 845-372-5770

NY STATE LIC. NO. 10491207973 // CORNWALL ON HUDSON, NY 12520

 INFO@ALMAXREALTY.COM

10 REASONS TO PLANT A TREE THIS SPRING

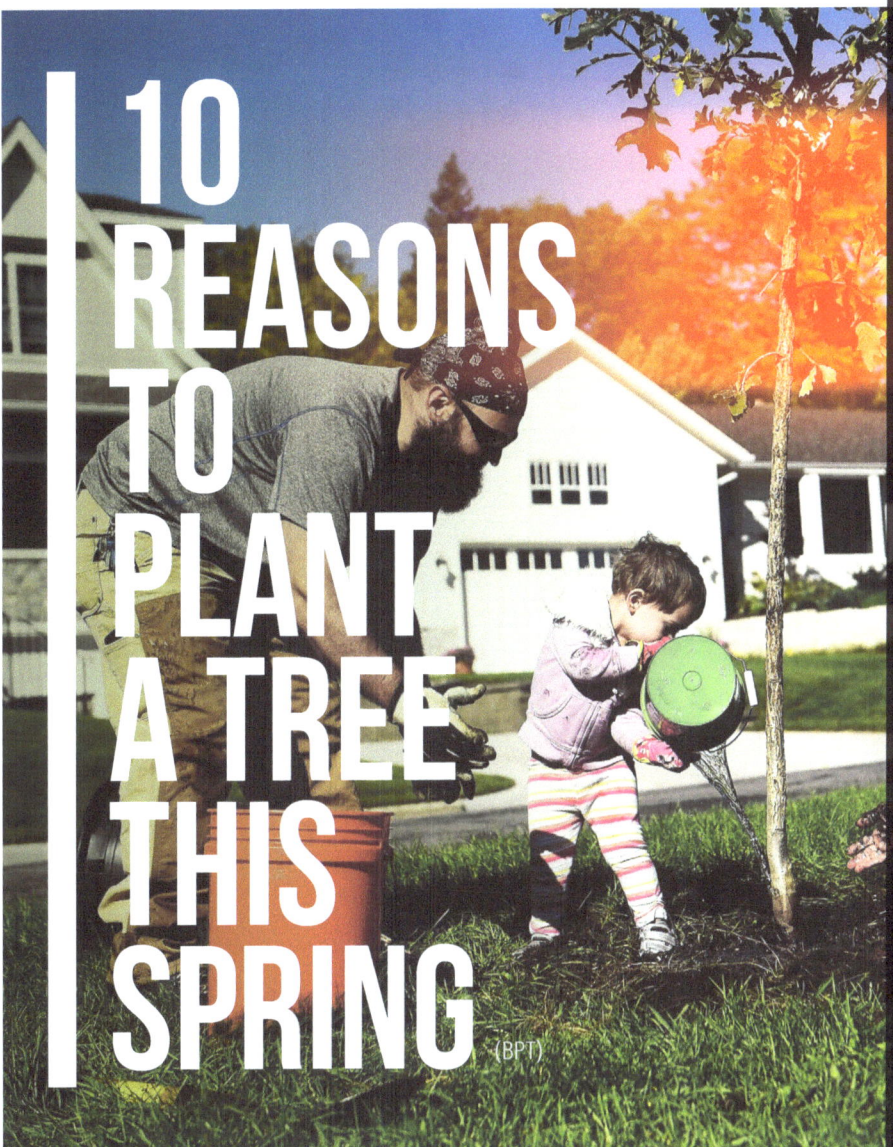

(BPT)

Did you know planting a tree is one of the easiest and most powerful things you can do to have a positive impact on the environment? It's true. Trees clean the air, prevent rainwater runoff, help you save energy and even combat global warming. And they're a snap to plant! No horticultural degree required. With Arbor Day just around the corner in April, there's no better time to give Mother Nature a little TLC by planting a tree.

From the single homeowner in Nebraska planting a maple in her backyard to the 250 Comcast employees volunteering in communities devastated by hurricanes, fires and Emerald Ash Borer infestation by planting hundreds of trees on Comcast Cares Day (the nation's largest single-day corporate volunteer event), people nationwide are getting their tree on this spring. Here are 10 reasons why you should join them.

■ TREES FIGHT CLIMATE CHANGE
Through photosynthesis, trees absorb harmful carbon dioxide, removing and storing the carbon and releasing oxygen back into the air.

■ TREES CLEAN THE AIR AND HELP YOU BREATHE
Trees don't just absorb CO2. They also absorb odors and pollutants like nitrogen oxides, ammonia, sulfur dioxide and ozone. It's estimated that one tree can absorb nearly 10 pounds of polluted air each year and release 260 pounds of oxygen.

■ TREES PREVENT SOIL EROSION AND RAINWATER RUNOFF
During heavy rains, water runoff finds its way to streams, lakes and wetlands, the potential for flooding plus picks up and carries pollutants along the way. Leaf canopies help buffer the falling rain and their roots hold the soil in place, encouraging the water to seep into the ground rather than run off.

■ PLANTING TREES IS EASY
Just choose a spot in your yard and you're good to go.

■ YOU'LL SAVE MONEY
Trees conserve energy in summer and winter, providing shade from the hot summer sun and shelter from cold winter winds.

■ TREES INCREASE YOUR HOME'S VALUE
Studies of comparable homes with and without trees show that, if you have trees in your yard, your home's value increases by up to 15 percent.

■ YOU'LL ATTRACT BIRDS
Trees provide nesting sites, food and shelter for your bird friends. Hang a feeder in one of the branches and enjoy the birdsong all year long.

■ TREES ARE GOOD FOR YOUR MENTAL AND PHYSICAL HEALTH
A view of trees in urban areas has been proven to reduce stress, anxiety and even the crime rate.

Planting Trees is a symbol of your commitment to the environment and the beauty of the world around you that will live on far beyond your own lifetime.

■ FREE TREES!
Join the nonprofit Arbor Day Foundation for $10 and they'll send you 10 trees selected for the region of the country where you live, at the right time to plant them. You'll also get planting instructions and other information. The trees are guaranteed to grow or the Foundation will replace them.

VISIT WWW.ARBORDAY.ORG TO JOIN.

REAL ESTATE PHOTOGRAPHY 101

61% MORE VIEWS ONLINE WITH PROFESSIONAL PHOTOS

UP TO 47% HIGHER ASKING PRICE/SQFT

80% OF BUYERS CITED THEY WOULDN'T EVEN CONSIDER A LISTING WITHOUT PHOTOGRAPHS

98% OF BUYERS THINK PROFESSIONAL PHOTOS ARE MOST USEFUL WHEN LOOKING FOR HOME ONLINE

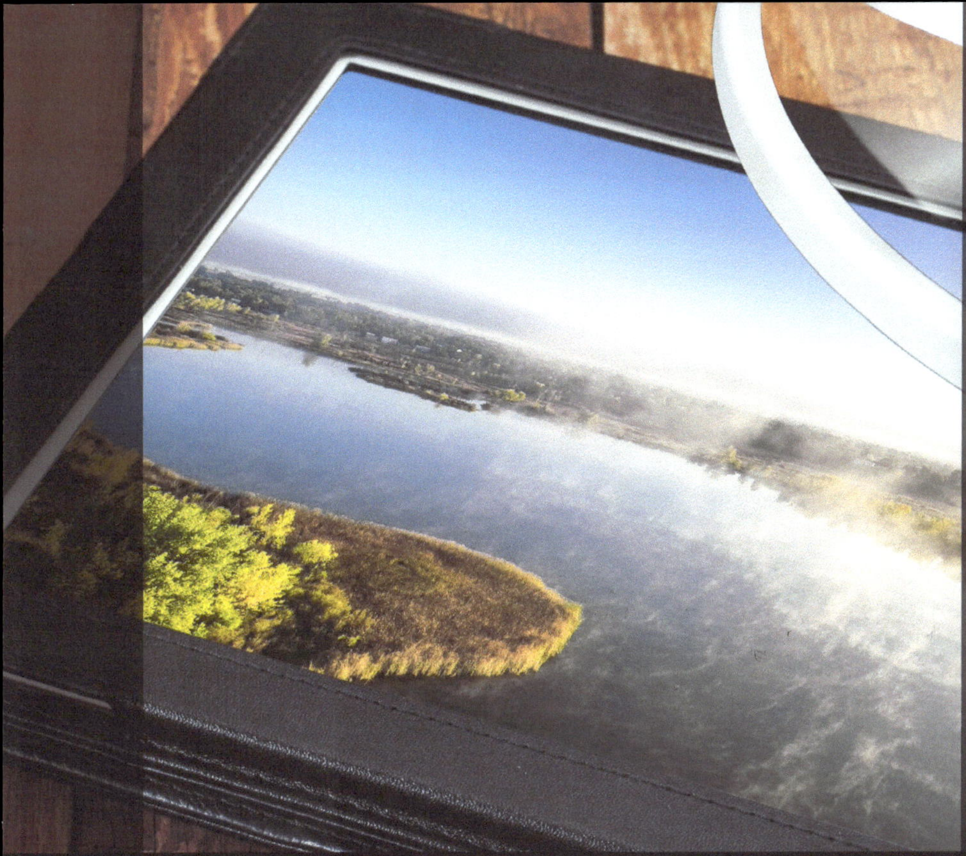

AERIAL & DRONE IMAGING

CONSIDER THESE HIGH-TECH UPGRADES

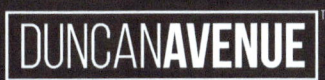
HUDSON VALLEY REAL ESTATE SERVICES

SCHEDULE YOUR PHOTOSHOOT @
DUNCANAVENUE.COM

STATISTICS SOURCE:
NATIONAL ASSOCIATION OF REALTORS

PROFESSIONAL LIGHTING
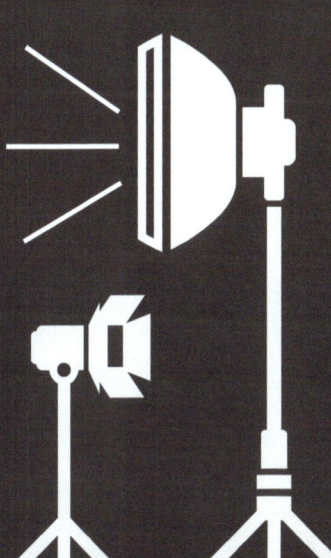

DSLR CAMERAS & LENSES
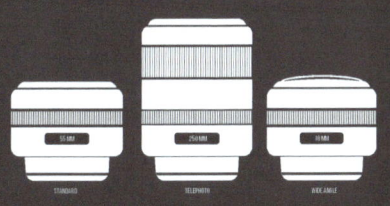
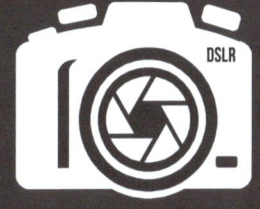

PROFESSIONAL RETOUCHING

+ DIGITAL STAGING
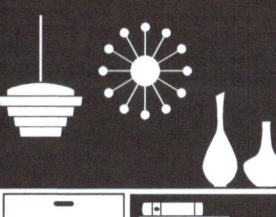

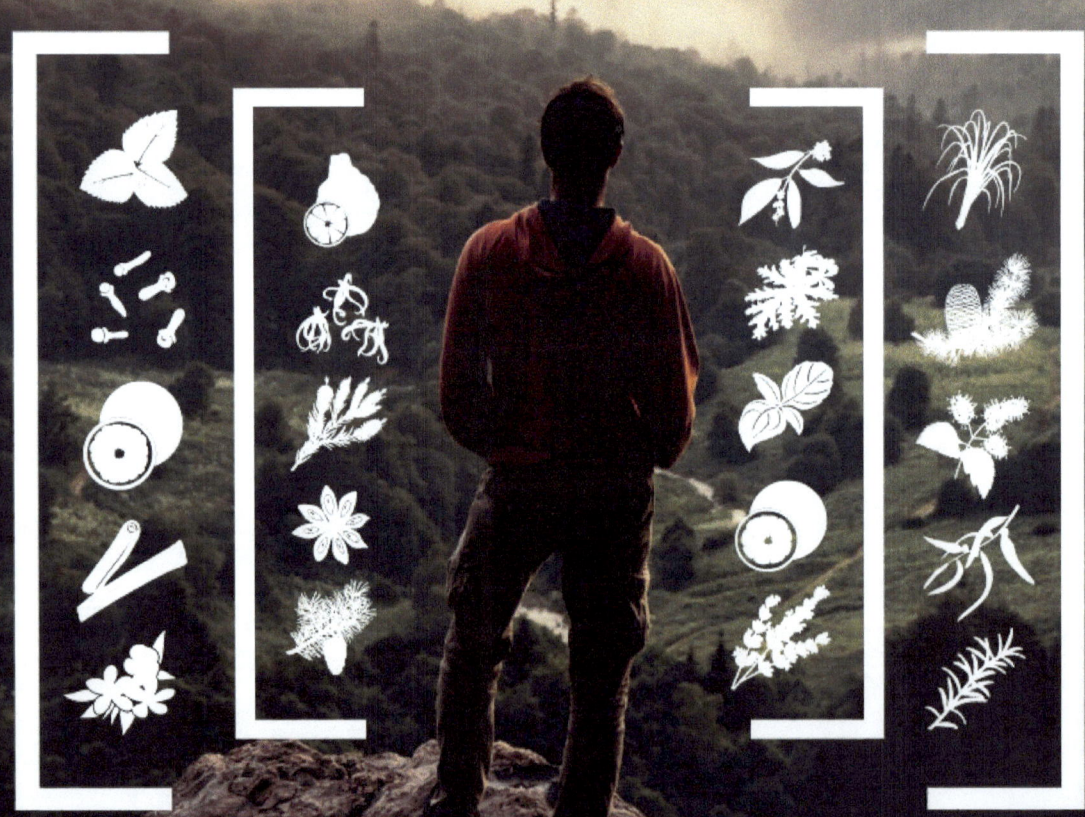

SPRING ESSENTIALS

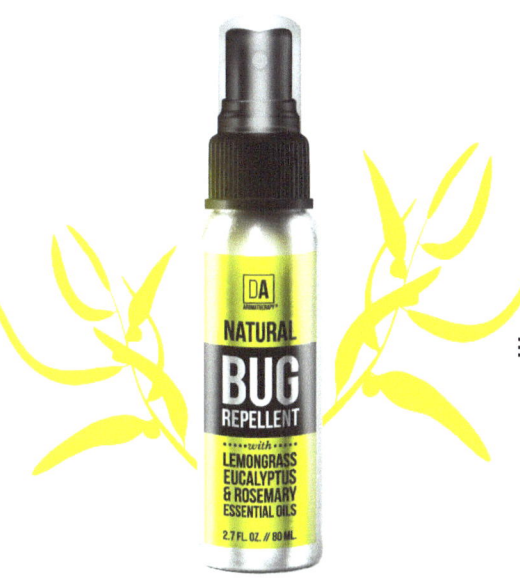

WOODLAND TRAILS BLEND
by DA Aromatherapy Collection

This natural insect repellent is made with 7 organic essential oils, it provides broad-spectrum protection and repels mosquitoes and ticks, fleas and many other pesky insects. The Best Natural Tick and Mosquito Repellent Spray is created for direct skin contact, safe for Humans and Pets and featuring exclusive Woodland Trails™ blend of Organic Lemongrass, Eucalyptus Lemon, and Eucalyptus Globulus, Cedarwood (Cedar Oil), Rosemary, Clove, and Lavender Essential Oils.

Our signature Tick and Mosquito Natural Spray will keep you sting and bite-free without the use of pesticides that are harmful to humans, the environment at large and especially good insects like honeybees. Our natural tick and mosquito repellent can help to protect you when sprayed in a room, on the balcony, in a car, on the body, and even on your clothes without staining.

DA-AROMATHERAPY.COM
$12.00

INSPIRING AROMATHERAPY MIST WITH ORGANIC LAVENDER AND SANDALWOOD ESSENTIAL OILS - WINDS OF STORMKING™
by DA Aromatherapy Collection

A luxurious and sensual fragrance of rich, woodsy sandalwood accord and beautiful flowery notes of lavender and spice. Winds of Stormking™ Essential Oil Blend perfectly captures the cool mountain breezes, sun sparkles in the Hudson River waters and lush foliage of the Hudson Valley.

DA-AROMATHERAPY.COM
$9.00

NATURAL HAND SANITIZERS WITH ORGANIC ESSENTIAL OILS
by DA Aromatherapy Collection

Flu season is here! Protect yourself and loved ones and get aromatherapy boost on the go with these natural hand sanitizers. DA Aromatherapy Hand Sanitizing Mists with Organic Essential Oils are effective against 99.9% of common germs and bacteria.

DA-AROMATHERAPY.COM
$9.00

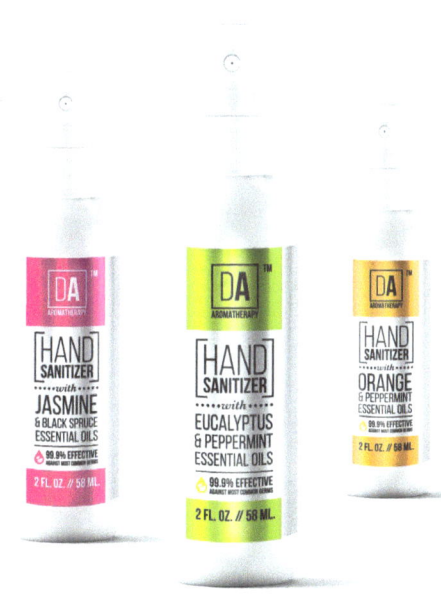

It's your home's focal point. The site of some of your best moments and the base of operations for entertaining - it's your kitchen, and no room in your home is more valuable. A magnificent kitchen defines a home, and bringing your kitchen to this level means capitalizing on today's top trends.

Many of the trends that will define kitchens for the year appear first at KBIS, the kitchen and bath industry convention held every year in January. More than 600 brands attended this year's event, and here are the five trends that stood out from the show and are sure to dictate kitchen styles for the rest of this year and beyond.

APPLIANCES THAT CAN DO IT ALL

As home chefs have become much more refined, the need for kitchen appliances capable of delivering to these expectations has increased. Signature Kitchen Suite, the new-to-the-scene luxury brand, for example, debuted the first-of-its-kind pro-style range with built-in sous vide for the ultimate in precision cooking. The range is among the most versatile available with two extra-high burners that deliver 23,000 BTUs of cooking power and two ultra-low burners to maintain temperatures as low as 100 degrees. This appliance is also Wi-Fi enabled, which means you can monitor and control your kitchen wherever you are.

UNIQUE BACKSPLASHES

The tile backsplash still has plenty of staying power, but the latest trends are upping the wow factor of this kitchen mainstay. From mirrored glass and backlit onyx to decorative sculptures, the kitchen backsplash is becoming the statement piece of any kitchen and a unique way to express your own style and taste.

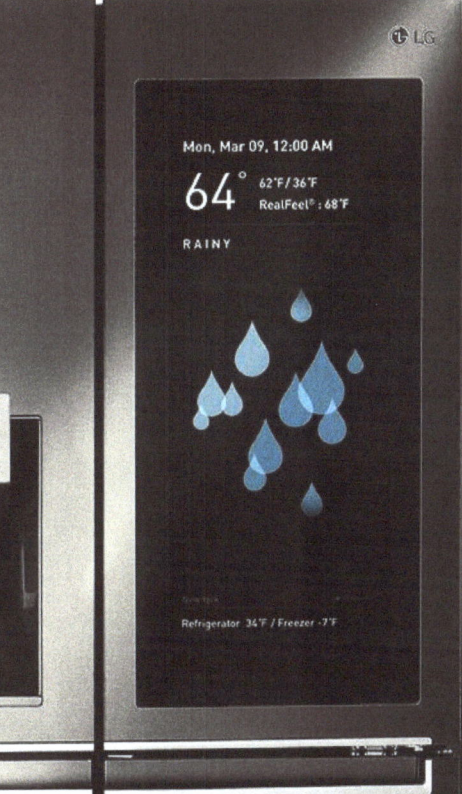

[SMART STYLE]

5 TOP TRENDS FOR YOUR KITCHEN IN 2018

(BPT)

MATTE BLACK FINISHES

The standard appearance of kitchen fixtures is taking on a darker tone in 2018, as matte black finishes are flourishing in a big way. This elegant, luxe appliance finish complements any kitchen and is also designed to conceal fingerprints and smudges. This smooth, low-gloss design option enhances any style kitchen, from modern to farmhouse, traditional to contemporary and every style in between.

DESIGN ELEMENTS

Long a place of functional purity, the kitchen is getting a dramatically artistic makeover in 2018. Designers from one side of KBIS to the other were showcasing lavish kitchens complemented with unique patterns, angles and texture choices. You simply wanted to go out and touch and savor every single detail they offered. The takeaway? It is possible to enjoy looking at your kitchen as much as you enjoy working in it.

[SMART STYLE]

SMARTER KITCHENS

New Wi-Fi enabled appliances are helping people control their homes in new ways, allowing for greater convenience - either through the touch of a button on their smartphone or via voice commands through Amazon Alexa and Google Assistant. Want to preheat the oven before you head home from work? Done! Need a fresh batch of ice before company arrives? You don't even have to get up. Forget to turn on the dishwasher? No problem. Choose a cycle and turn it on from virtually anywhere. Smart home leaders like LG have also teamed with food and recipe services such as Innit and SideChef to better assist home chefs with planning, shopping, preparing and cooking delicious meals.

Taking your kitchen to the next level The latest and greatest innovations for your kitchen were on display at KBIS, but bringing them home is up to you. Need more renovation inspiration? Check out new virtual design tools to experiment with different styles and appliance combinations to create your dream kitchen. You may just find a whole new look for your kitchen.

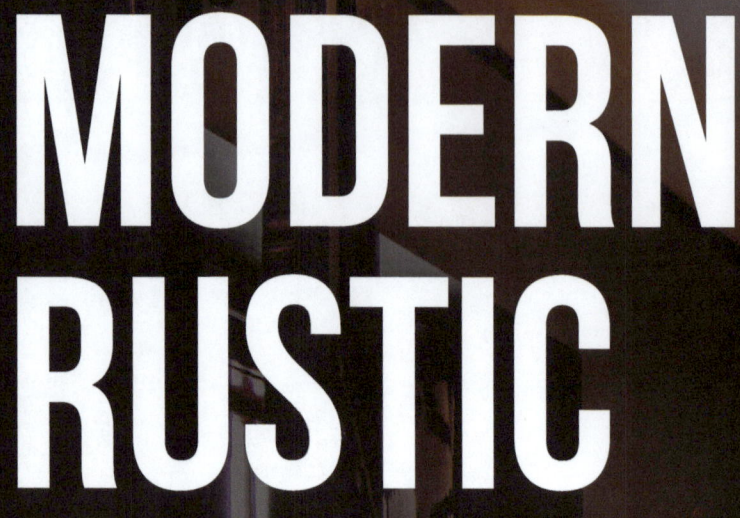

MODERN RUSTIC

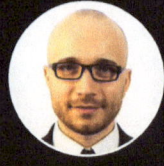

PRINCE RESIDENCE // NEWBURGH, NY
PHOTO STORY BY MAXWELL ALEXANDER

EVOLUTION OF THE HUDSON VALLEY STYLE

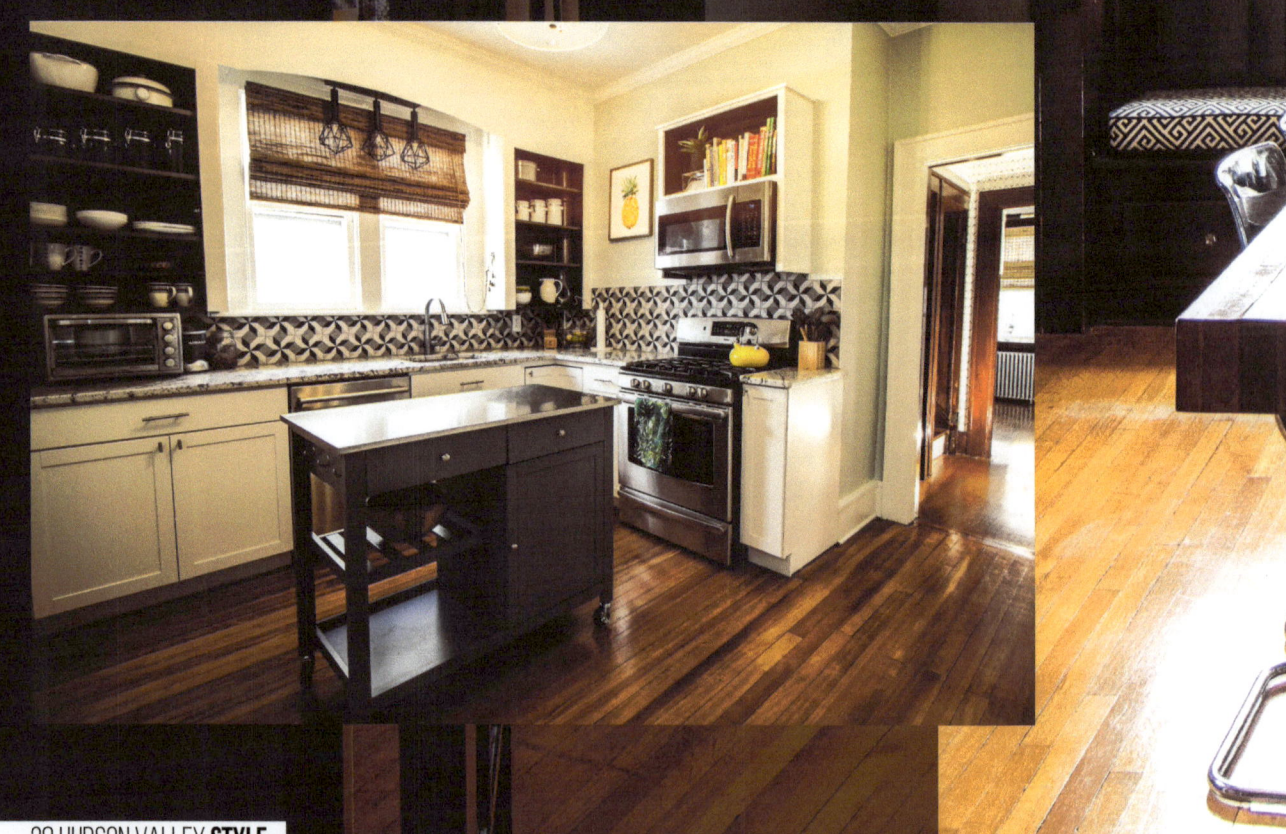

[HUDSON VALLEY STYLE INTERIORS]

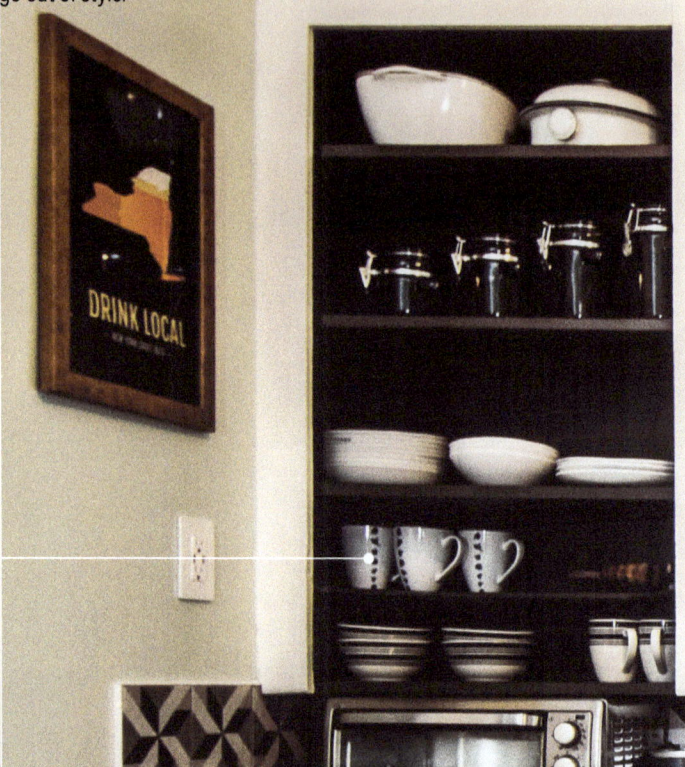

[**GEOMETRIC PATTERNS & SHAPES**

Always classy in black & white, geometric patterns give the space contemporary yet timeless & trendy look. Design is intelligence made visible and that will never go out of style.

[**ECO-CONSCIOUS FINISHES**

Natural materials like stainless steel, wood, ceramics and concrete are a healthier choice and create significantly lower carbon footprint compared to plastics and polymers.

ANATOMY OF A GREAT KITCHEN DESIGN

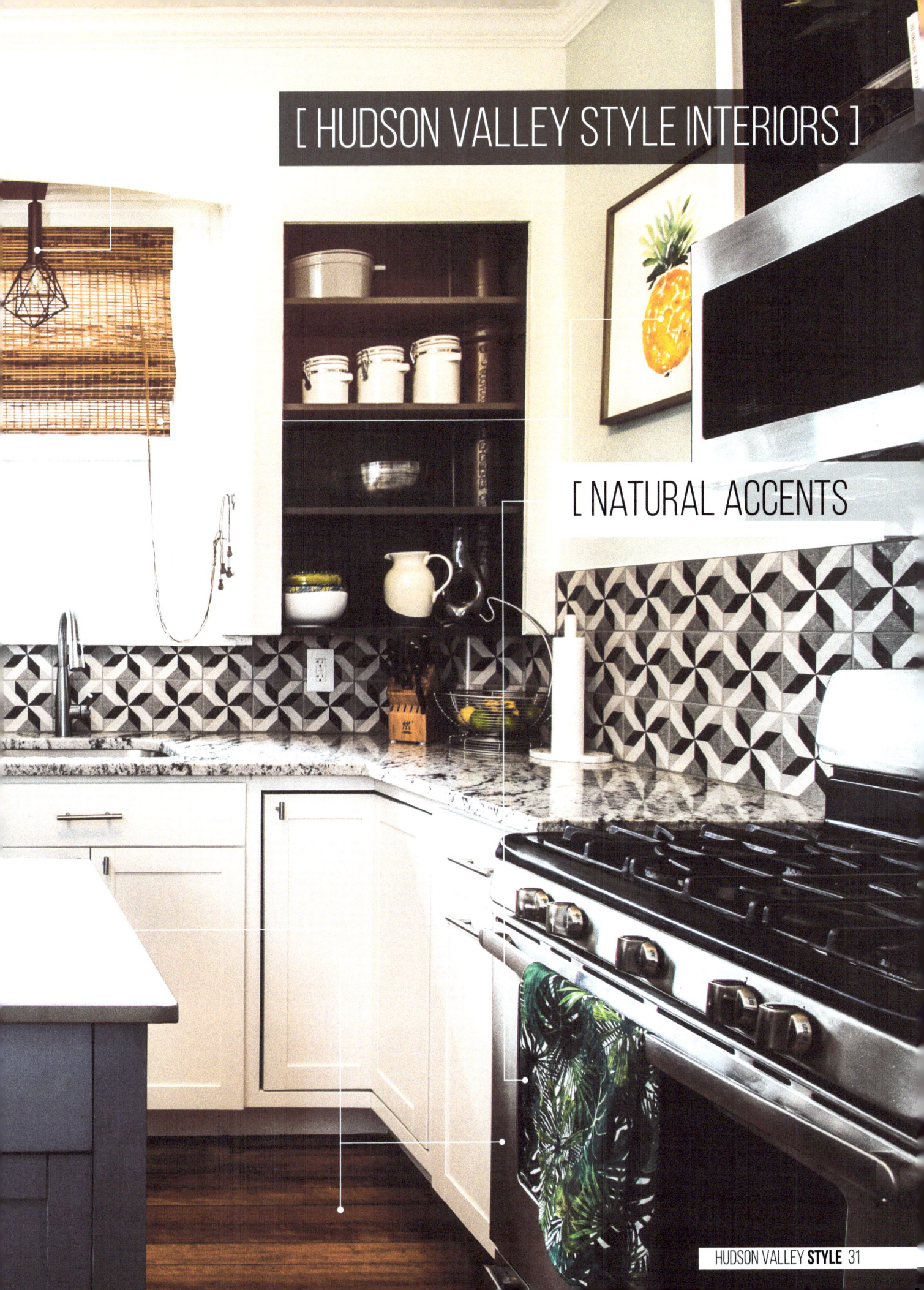

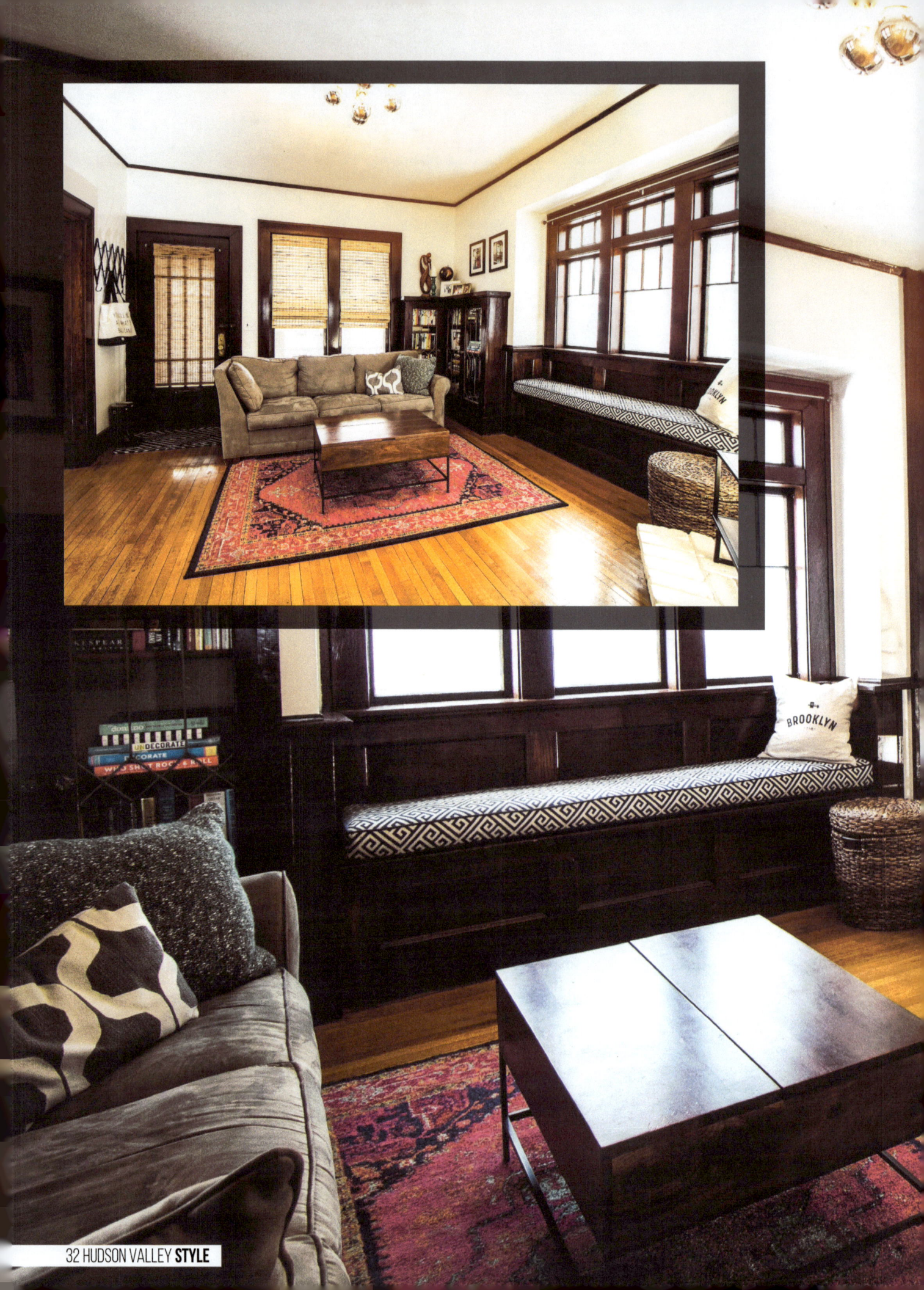

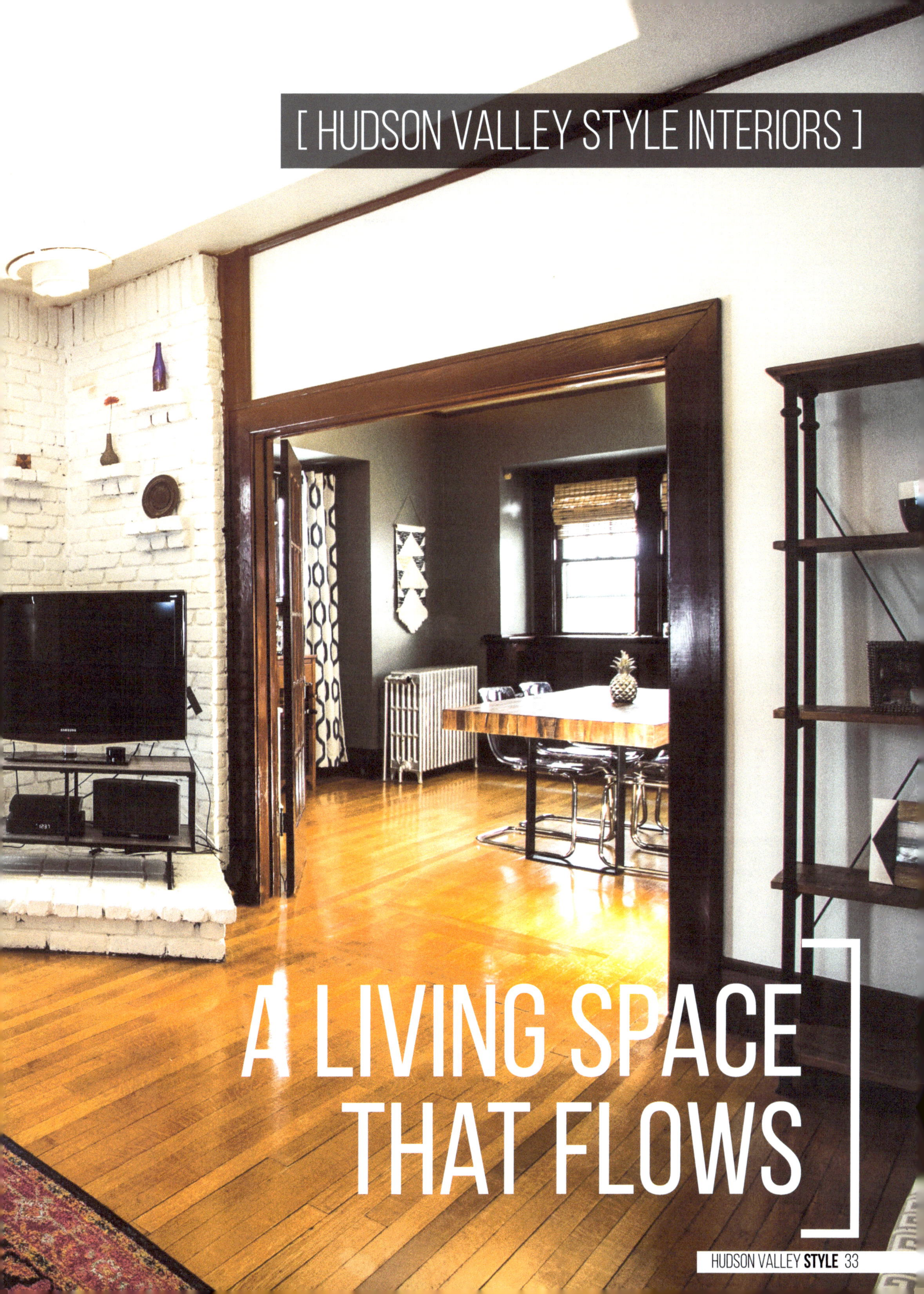

[HUDSON VALLEY STYLE INTERIORS]

A LIVING SPACE THAT FLOWS

[STYLE IMPROVEMENT]

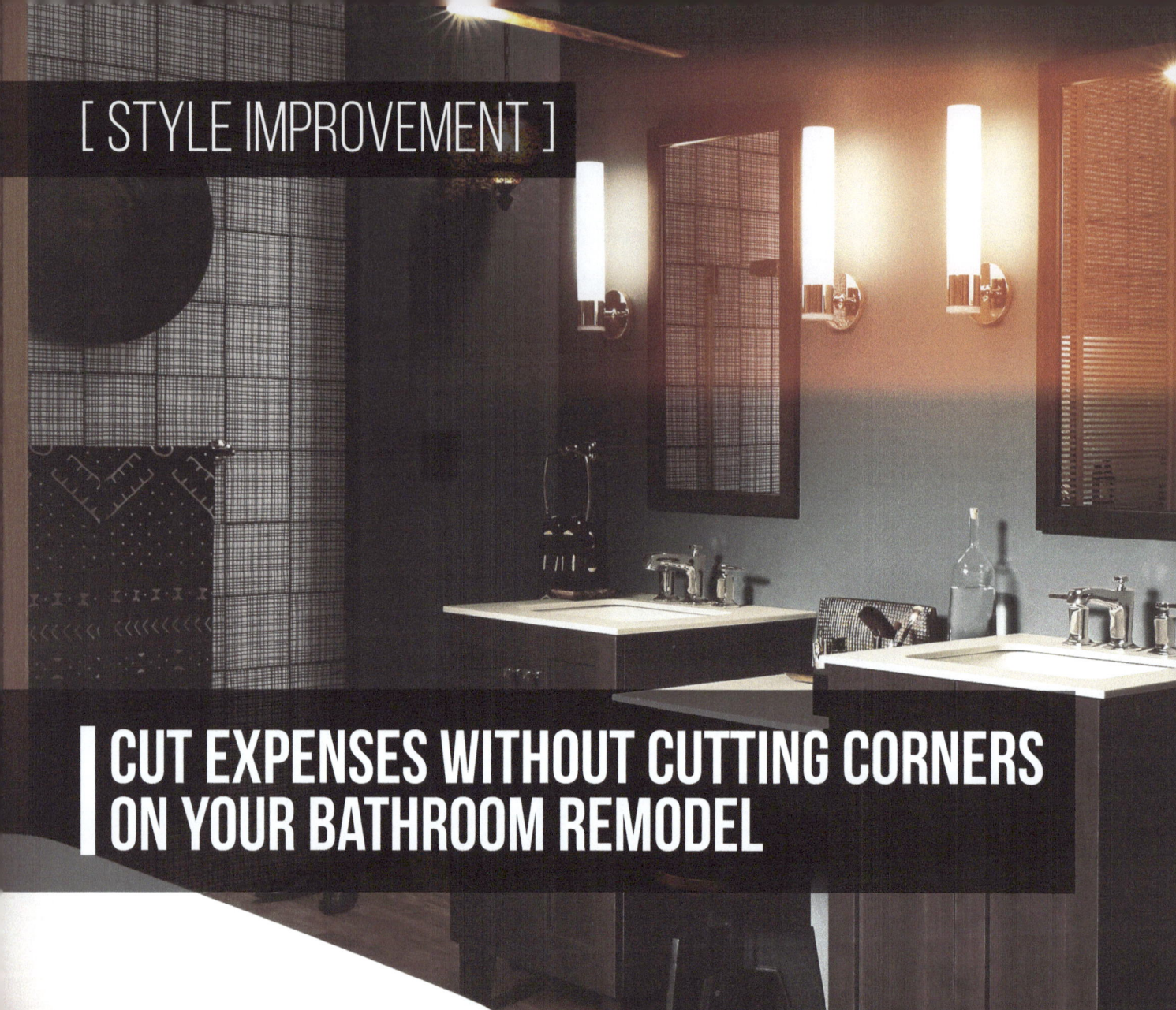

CUT EXPENSES WITHOUT CUTTING CORNERS ON YOUR BATHROOM REMODEL

(BPT) - When homeowners get the urge to remodel and renovate their homes, two rooms immediately top the list: the kitchen and the bathroom. In the last decade, we've seen something of a renaissance in home bathroom design. From an innovative use of materials to radically reimagined bathtubs and toilets, today's bathrooms offer a dream space with comfort and convenience in a stylish package.

This dream, however, comes with a price tag. A mid-range bathroom remodel that includes a steel tub, a pressure-balanced shower, ceramic tile floor, vanity and integral sink could cost almost $20,000, and that's for a 5-by-7 room. An upscale remodel might cost as much as $60,000!

But before this sticker shock scares you away, know there are secrets to saving money and still getting a beautiful bathroom. We sat down with Lynn Schrage, interior designer at Kohler Co. to learn some of her tips and tricks. Here are five of the best.

1. FIND A FOCAL POINT

You don't need to have top-of-the-line everything to create a stunning bathroom. Think in terms of what piece you want to be the star of your bathroom. Maybe you want it to be the sink, a freestanding bathtub or a spa steam shower. Pick one fixture that will draw the eye in and take center stage. You'll be amazed at what this does for the overall effect.

2. INCORPORATE CREATIVE STORAGE SOLUTIONS

In remodeling a bathroom, it's always exciting to stumble upon a solution that brings together the practical and the beautiful. This happens a lot when you try to figure out how to store toiletries, towels and more. Wall cabinets, wicker baskets, storage ladders and storage towers create charm and keep your essentials orderly.

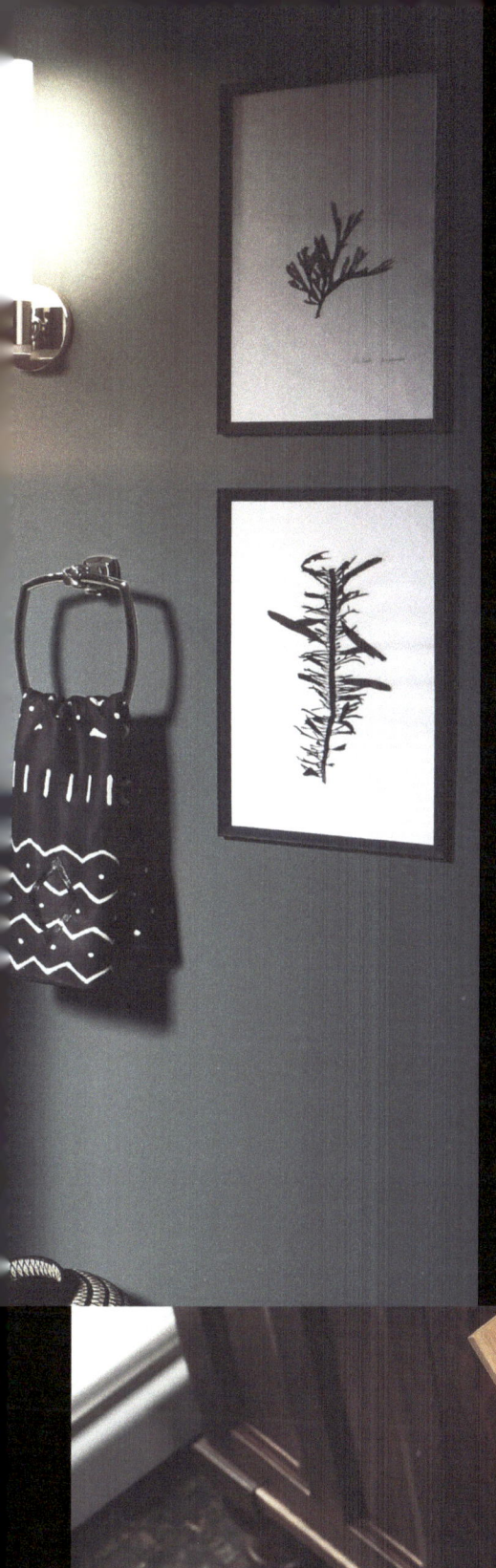

3. A TOUCH OF LUXURY GOES A LONG WAY

One of the most effective ways to create a stunning overall effect is to mix a touch of luxury with quality materials. For instance, coordinate wooden cabinets with a tiled paneling treatment around the bathroom. Also ripe for coordination are choreograph shower panels with stone or porcelain tiles. Focusing and investing in these luxury elements while using quality material will help offset costs and give you the look you've dreamed of.

4. SELECT AN INTEGRATED VANITY TOP SINK

Looking through your many choices of sinks, showerheads, toilets and other fixtures is downright inspiring, but sometimes it can be hard to know where to start. Of all the options available, consider setting your eye on a vanity top with sink mounted on any number of vanity styles you like. This combines style with functionality in a timeless design and cuts down on clean up and your installation cost.

5. WORK WITH A PROFESSIONAL

Many people who want to save on a bathroom remodel think the most economical way is to go it alone and take the DIY route. However, a professional designer can help you discover the style that fits your personality and budget - and help you avoid costly mistakes. For instance, Kohler's Bathroom Design Service provides expert advice, 3-D bathroom renderings and logistical guidance.

To discover more inspiration for your bathroom, visit ideas.kohler.com, where you'll find the ideas and advice that will get you started on your journey to your dream bathroom.

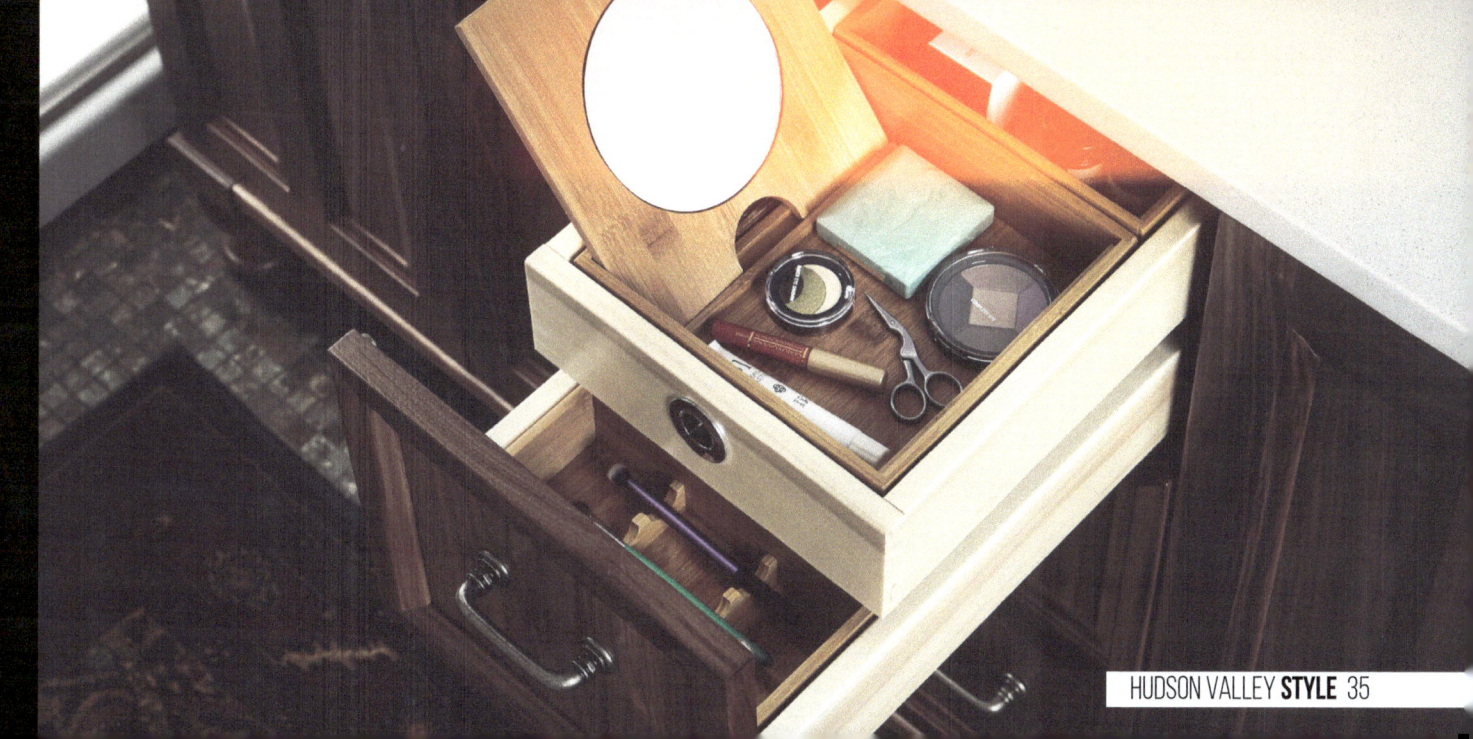

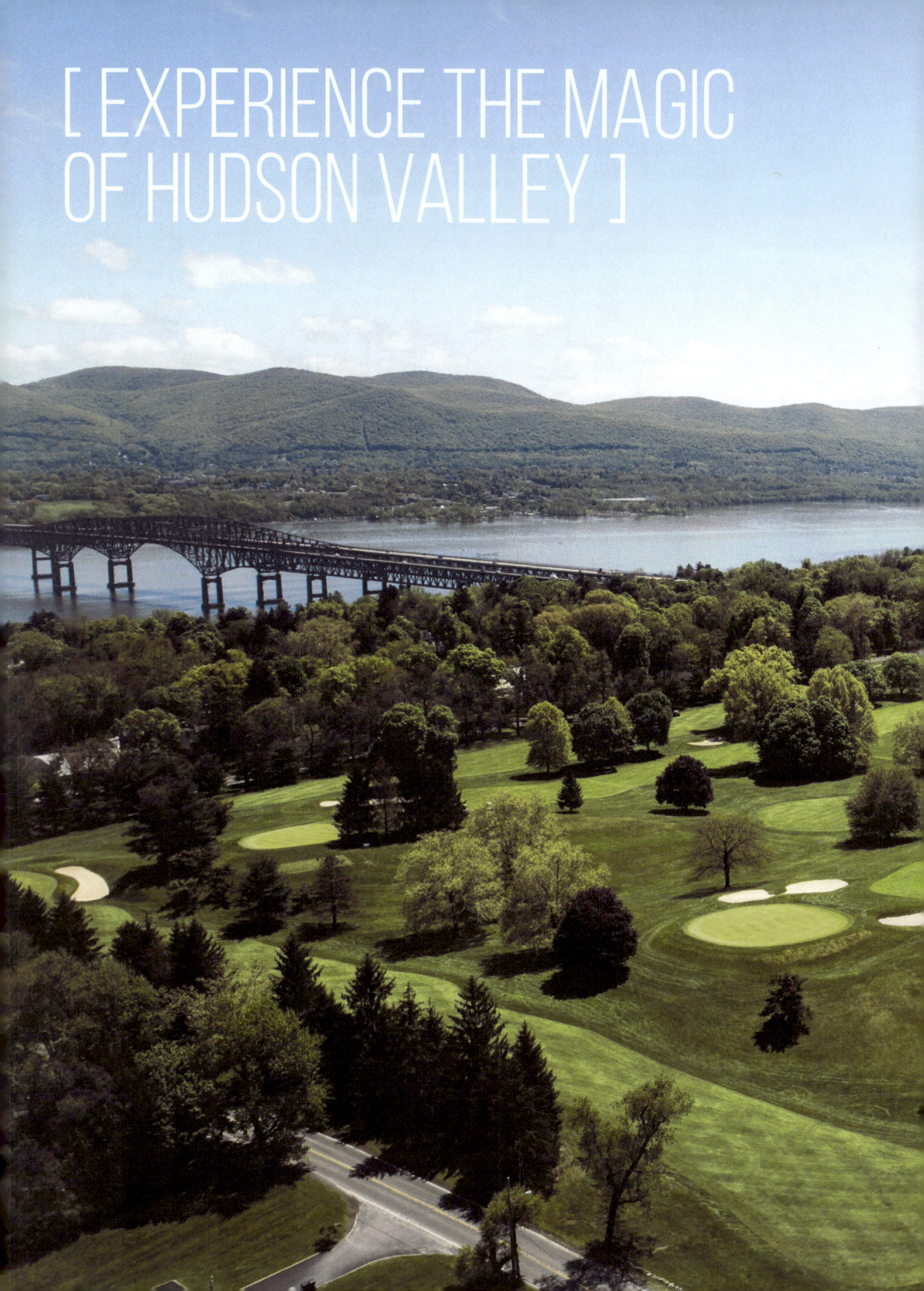

[EXPERIENCE THE MAGIC OF HUDSON VALLEY]

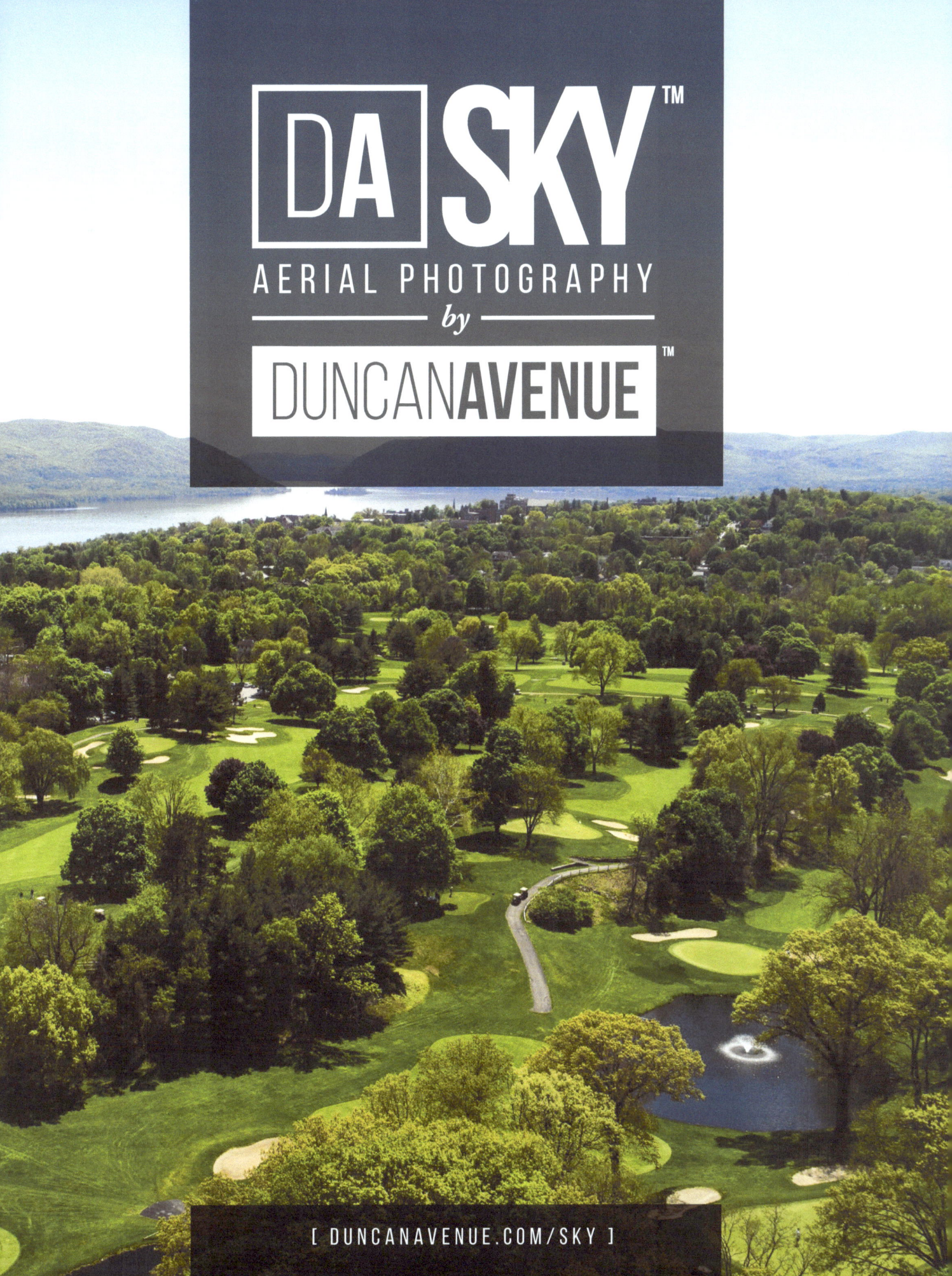

SELLING REAL ESTATE IN STYLE

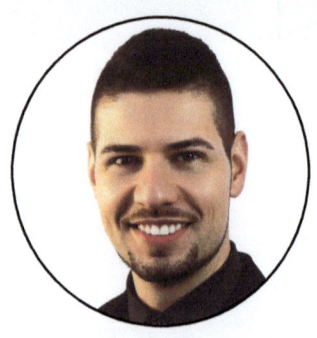

By Dino Alexander
(New York State Licensed Real Estate Broker)

Want to sell your home quickly and for top dollar? Staging with Style can help. Staging is presenting your home in its best and most appealing light to the majority of home-buyers.

In theory, staging isn't hard or costly, but in reality, many homeowners find it difficult because it's often hard to see something objectively when we love it.

An easy way to see effectively staged homes is to visit decorated models. Decorating a model is expensive, but builders are willing to invest the cost because they understand just how well a staged home sells. You too can profit from this knowledge.

Why do some sellers balk at staging their home? They think it's too expensive, they think it's too much work, they like their decorating, and they don't understand the value.

Expensive? Decorating with Style is not nearly as much as your first price reduction.

Work? Mostly cleaning and de-cluttering which you would have to do anyway since you're moving.

Decorating? Liking your decorating is understandable. Look at it this way – interior design is for living in your home, staging is for selling your home. They are distinctly different.

Value? Okay, there's the catch. How much does it really do for me?

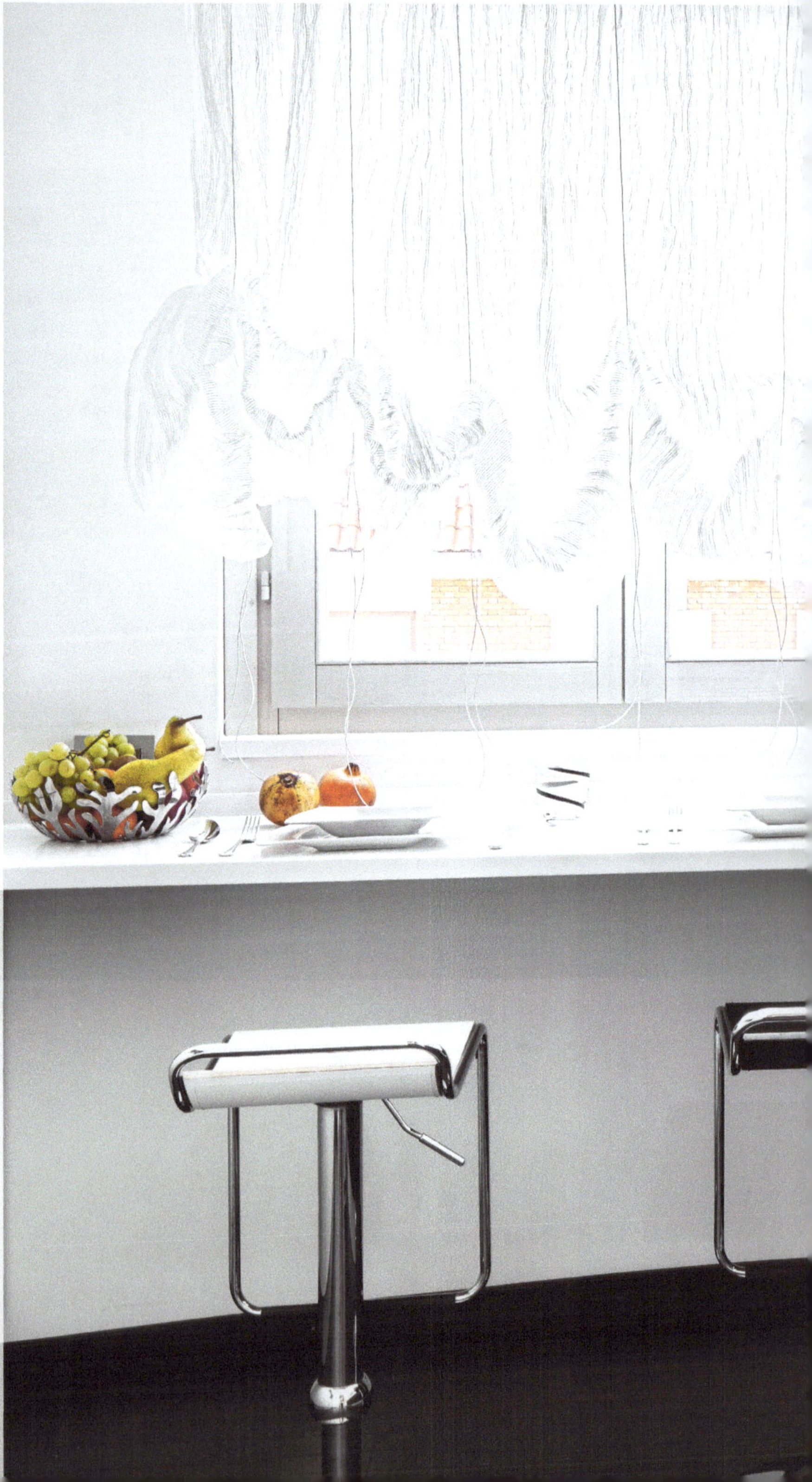

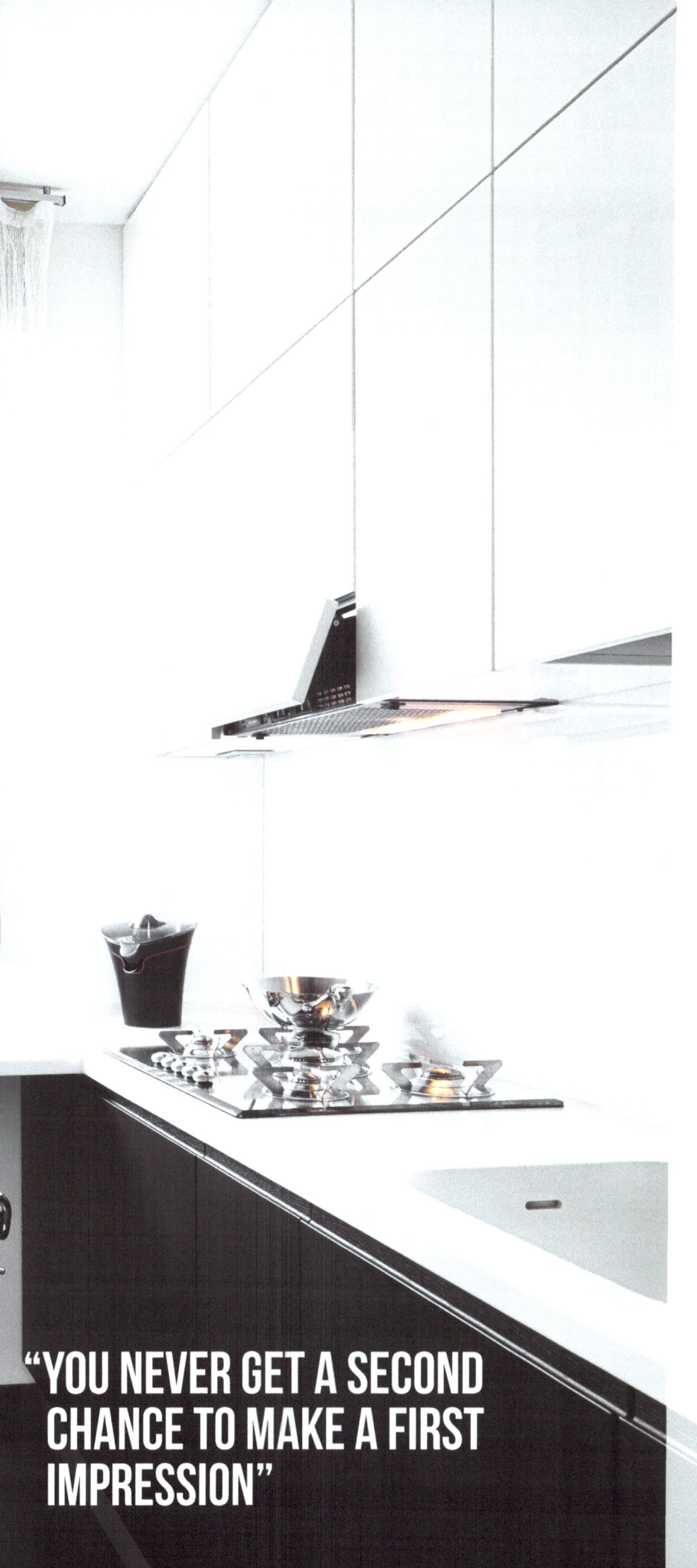

"YOU NEVER GET A SECOND CHANCE TO MAKE A FIRST IMPRESSION"

WHY IT IS IMPORTANT TO STAGE A HOUSE BEFORE SELLING IT:

- Get the Highest Price for Your Home. A well-staged home is aesthetically pleasing. Everything looks inviting, comfortable, and simple. It elicits a strong emotion from buyers: desire.

- Your Home Will Sell Faster – The Association of Property Scene Designers states that staged homes sell for 43% more quickly than unstaged homes.

- Staging Helps with Procrastination – yes, your stager will want many of your collector items put away. This is called de-cluttering and depersonalizing. You will have to tackle this at some point. Get it done early, store boxes in the basement, a POD, or rent a storage unit for a few months.

- Staging will teach you a Few Things. Maybe you never had a decorator and you've done it all yourself. Those floral curtains in the bedroom, the layout of the pictures over the living room sofa, the furniture placement in the family room or the overlarge chair in the den. It all works for you which is great – but a stager might just show you "better" which is something you can take with you to your new home.

- You Never Get a Second Chance to Make a First Impression – is a favorite line with stagers and real estate agents. If you don't stage before you list, guess what? You've lost time and money – the two things that are all but promised if you stage your home before listing it for sale.

- You get a good feeling when you walk into a home that has been properly staged. It's not fake, it's more than just place mats and wine glasses on the dining room table. It just feels good.

HUDSON VALLEY **STYLE** 39

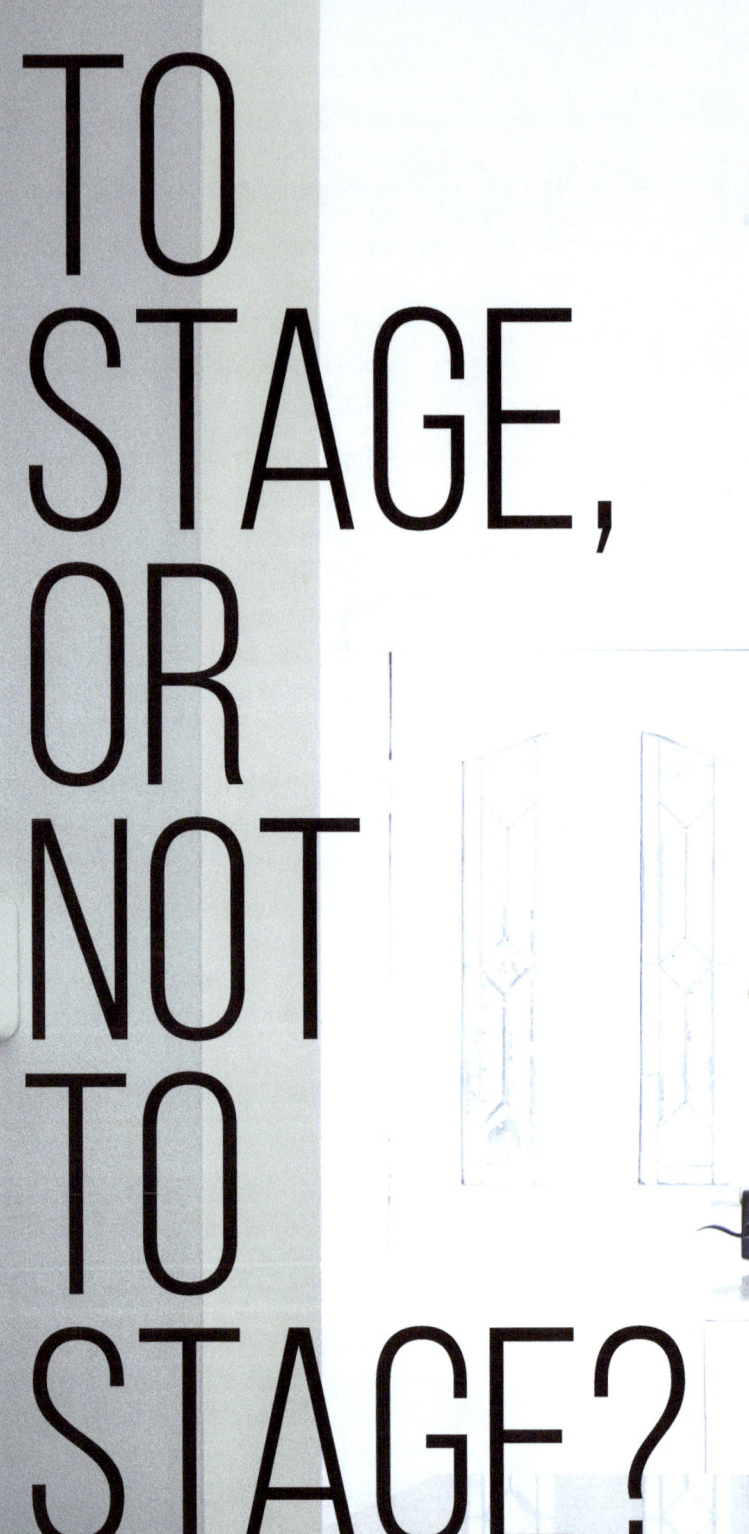

TO STAGE, OR NOT TO STAGE?

Learn More about this design project →
at duncanavenue.com/design

STAGED HOMES SELL 79% FASTER

STAGED HOMES SOLD IN 11 DAYS OR LESS
ON AVERAGE SPEND **73% LESS TIME ON THE MARKET**
(COMPARED TO AVERAGE 50 DAYS ON THE MARKET)

81% OF BUYERS
FIND THAT STAGING HELPS THEM BETTER **VISUALIZE A PROPERTY AS THEIR FUTURE HOME**

HIGHER SALES PRICES
STAGED HOMES SELL FOR **17% MORE** THAN NON-STAGED HOMES

BUYERS MOST OFTEN offer 1%-5% increase on the REAL VALUE OF A STAGED HOME

SELLERS SPEND LESS THAN 1% FOR STAGING SERVICES to get a 1000% RETURN ON INVESTMENT

HOME STAGING CAN BOOST PERCEIVED VALUE OF A HOME BY 20%

95% OF BUYER'S AGENTS SAY THAT HOME STAGING HAS A POSITIVE EFFECT ON THE HOME BUYER'S VIEW OF THE PROPERTY

3% YET LESS THAN 3% OF HOMES LISTED ON MLS ARE STAGED

DUNCAN AVENUE™
HUDSON VALLEY REAL ESTATE SERVICES

SCHEDULE YOUR CONSULTATION @
DUNCANAVENUE.COM

STATISTICS SOURCE:
NATIONAL ASSOCIATION OF REALTORS

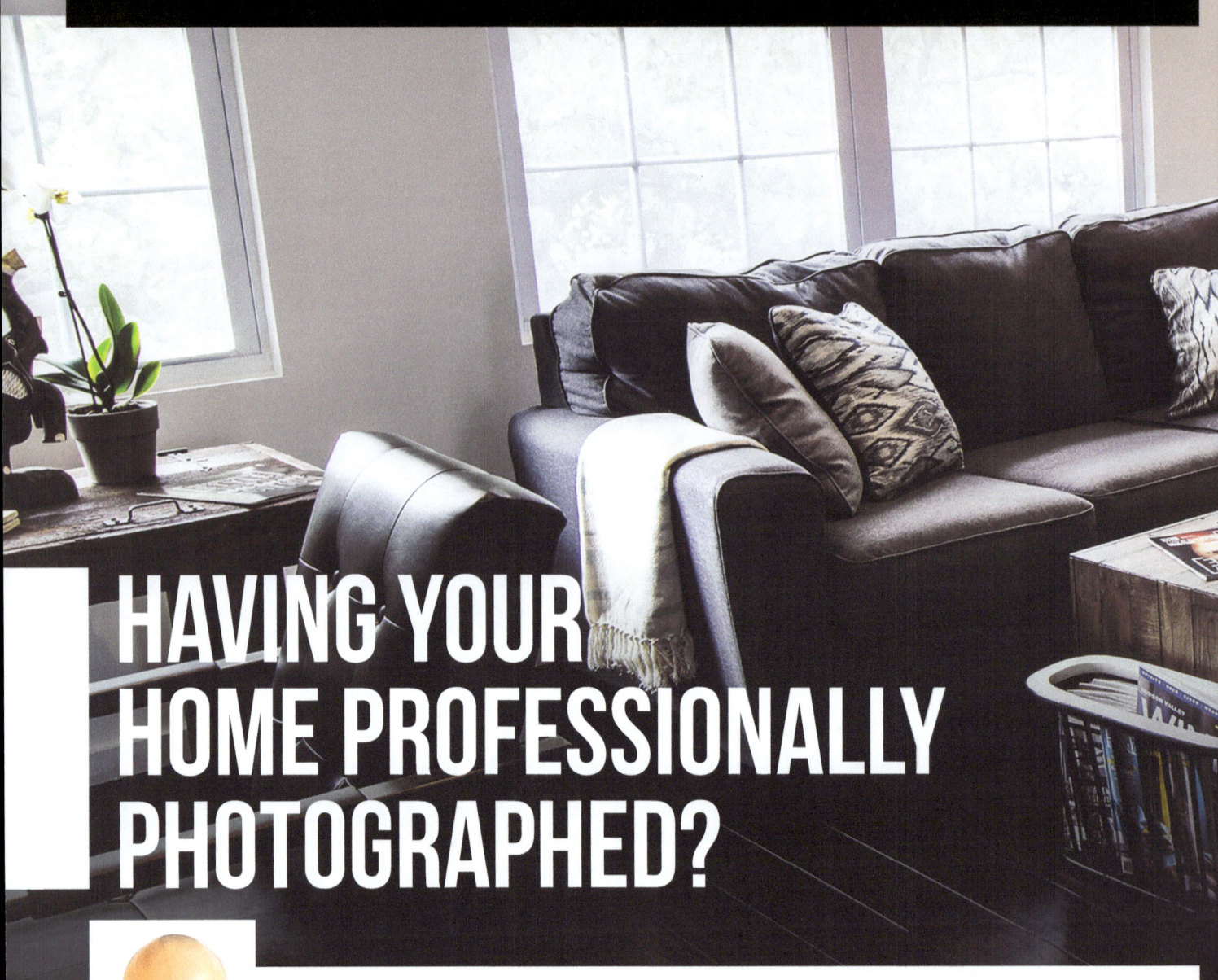

HAVING YOUR HOME PROFESSIONALLY PHOTOGRAPHED?

by **Maxwell Alexander,** President, Chief Design Officer, Duncan Avenue Group

The real estate market in the Hudson Valley and around the Globe has been changing rapidly, and that has created some challenges for home sellers. It was not that long ago that searching for a home meant driving from New York City all the way to beautiful Hudson Valley neighborhoods, picking up flyers and sales packets and maybe stumbling upon on open house or two.

In the 21st century, home searches are more likely to start online while at lunch break in the office than in the family car. The ease of browsing real estate listings online is hard to beat, and potential buyers can scour dozens of listings in the time it would take to visit just one in person.

The shift to online home shopping has created both challenges and opportunities. If you understand how home buyers shop and what they are looking for, then you can make your listing stand out and rise above the rest. If you fail to put your home in its best light, would-be buyers could pass your home by as they do their online shopping.

Hiring a local Hudson Valley professional photographer is one of the best ways to make your home stand out. Duncan Avenue Real Estate Photography Studio is your premier professional photography provider in the Hudson Valley area including Orange, Rockland, Dutchess, Ulster, Putnam, Westchester, Greene, Rensselaer, Columbia, Saratoga and Albany Counties. We'll take care of making your online photographs stand out, but there are certain things you should do before the pro arrives. Here are the steps you should take while you wait for the photographer.

| SECURE YOUR PETS

If you have a dog that is aggressive, territorial or just protective, be sure to secure the animal long before the photographer is scheduled to arrive. We love dogs, and in fact we've got two super hyper Jack Russell Terriers at home, however they could definitely get in a way of making your home look good in the pictures, especially if they are so cute that it's just way too distracting.

Even if your pets are not too aggressive, they could get in the way during the photo shoot. Placing your cats and dogs in the basement or garage is a courtesy you should extend to the professional who will be photographing your home.

| START A FIRE

If your home has a fireplace, we would want to show it off. Be sure you have a roaring fire going in each of your fireplaces before the

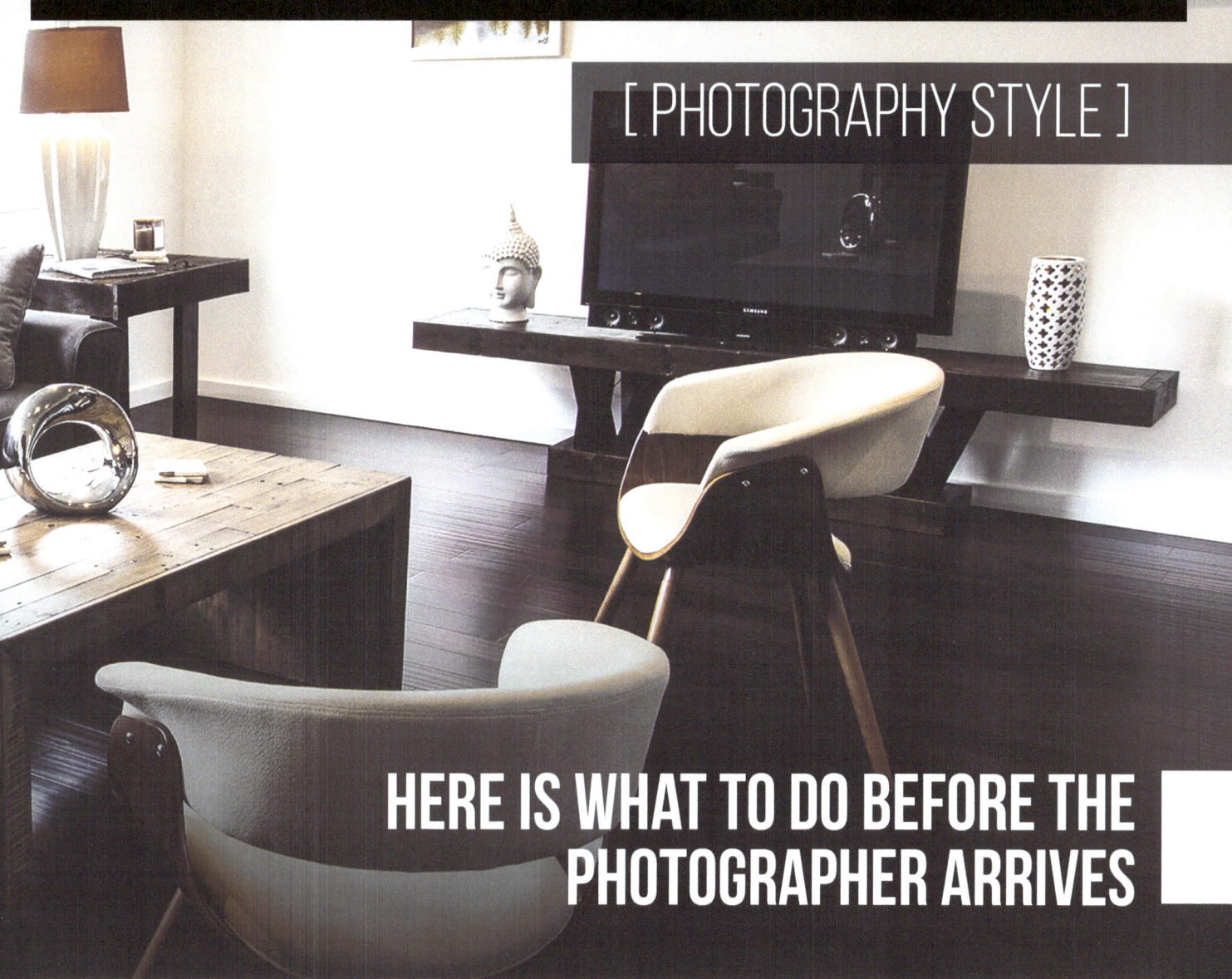

[PHOTOGRAPHY STYLE]

HERE IS WHAT TO DO BEFORE THE PHOTOGRAPHER ARRIVES

photographer arrives.

A lit fireplace will not only make your home look inviting, but it also serves as proof that it's working correctly. A fireplace can be a big selling point, so do not sell yourself short.

| LIGHT SOME CANDLES

You can create a homey and inviting environment even if your home does not have a fireplace. Just pick your favorite candles, scatter them around the house and light them up when the photographer arrives.

A set of tapers on the table will create a romantic setting and make your finished photographs look great. A large pillar candle in the living room will create an inviting atmosphere and encourage browsers to take a look. Use your imagination, and ask your Hudson Valley Real Estate Photography Pro for other lighting ideas when he arrives.

| LIGHT IT UP

Speaking of lighting, turn all the lights on before the photographer's scheduled arrival. If any light bulbs are burned out, take the time to replace them. Set the dimmers to full power so that your home looks as bright and airy as possible.

You can let even more light in by rolling up the blinds and opening up the curtains. You want the space to be as bright and inviting as possible, and that brightness will come through in the finished photographs.

We will bring supplemental lighting with us to make sure all areas of your home look the best they can.

| CLEAR OUT THE DRIVEWAY

We would want shots of the driveway, so remove any cars, trucks or other vehicles before the scheduled photo shoot. Be sure to park them well down the street, keeping the road in front of your home open as possible. Duncan Avenue Photography Studio is the only Real Estate Photography Studio that offers complementary FAA-licensed aerial/drone photography with every property or listing package.

Staging your home for open houses and private showings is important, but making your home look great in the listing photographs may be even more important. You can think of your listing photographs as a special kind of staging, one designed to draw the eyes of would-be buyers and get them to schedule a private appointment.

Make your appointment today at DuncanAvenue.com

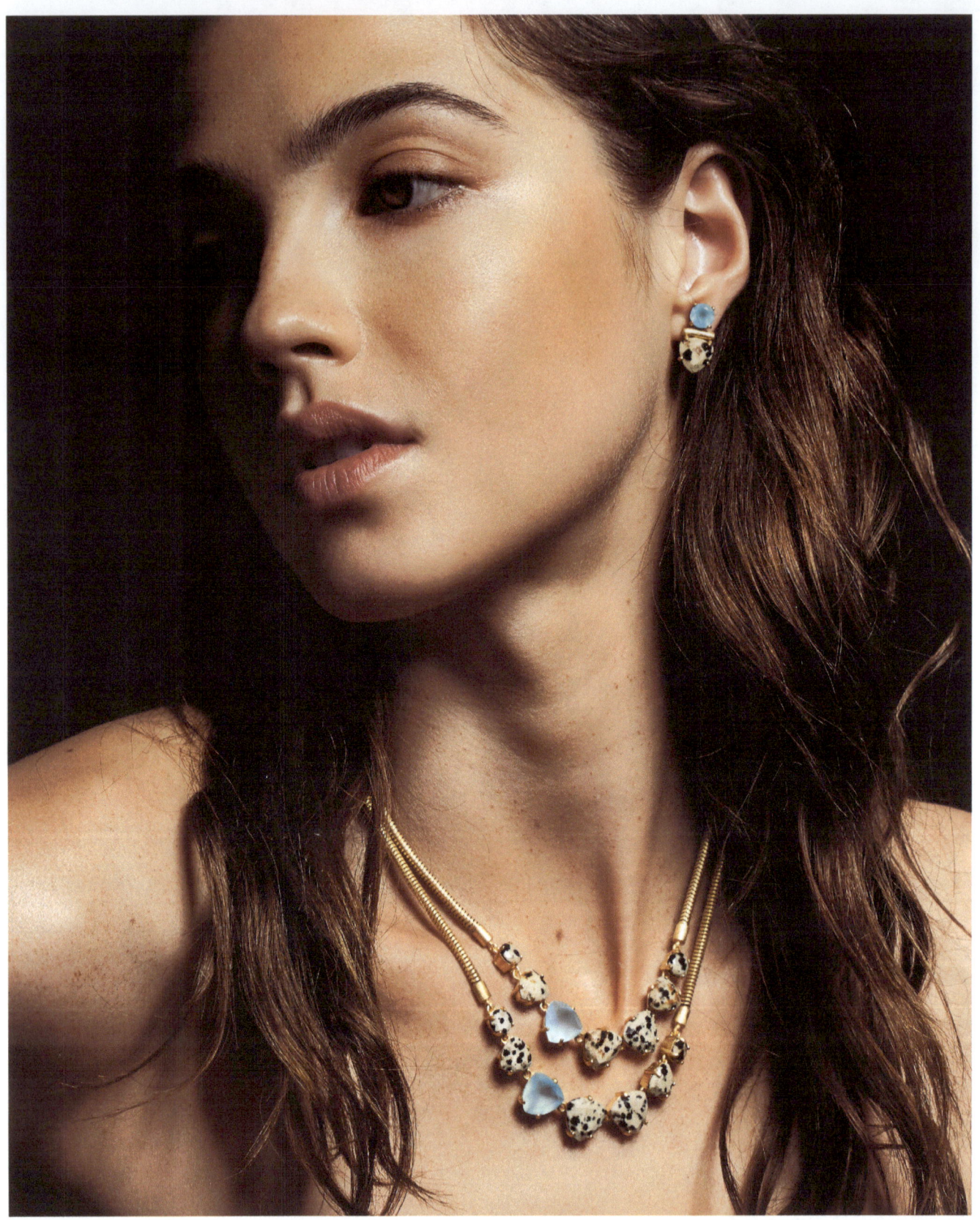

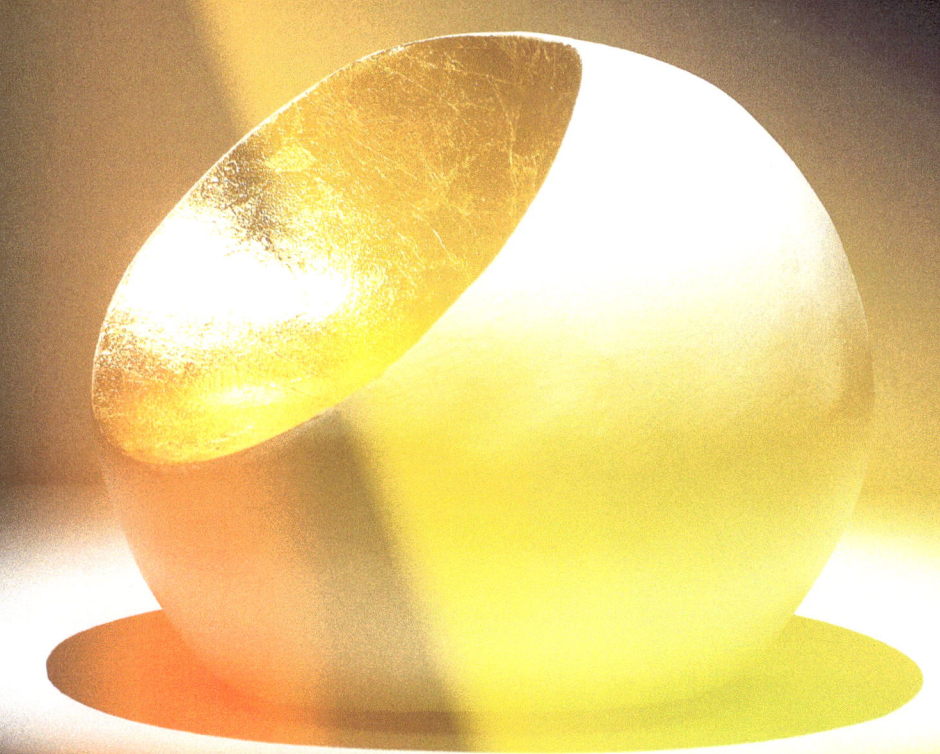

MAXWELL ALEXANDER |DESIGN™
maxwellalexander.design/sculpture

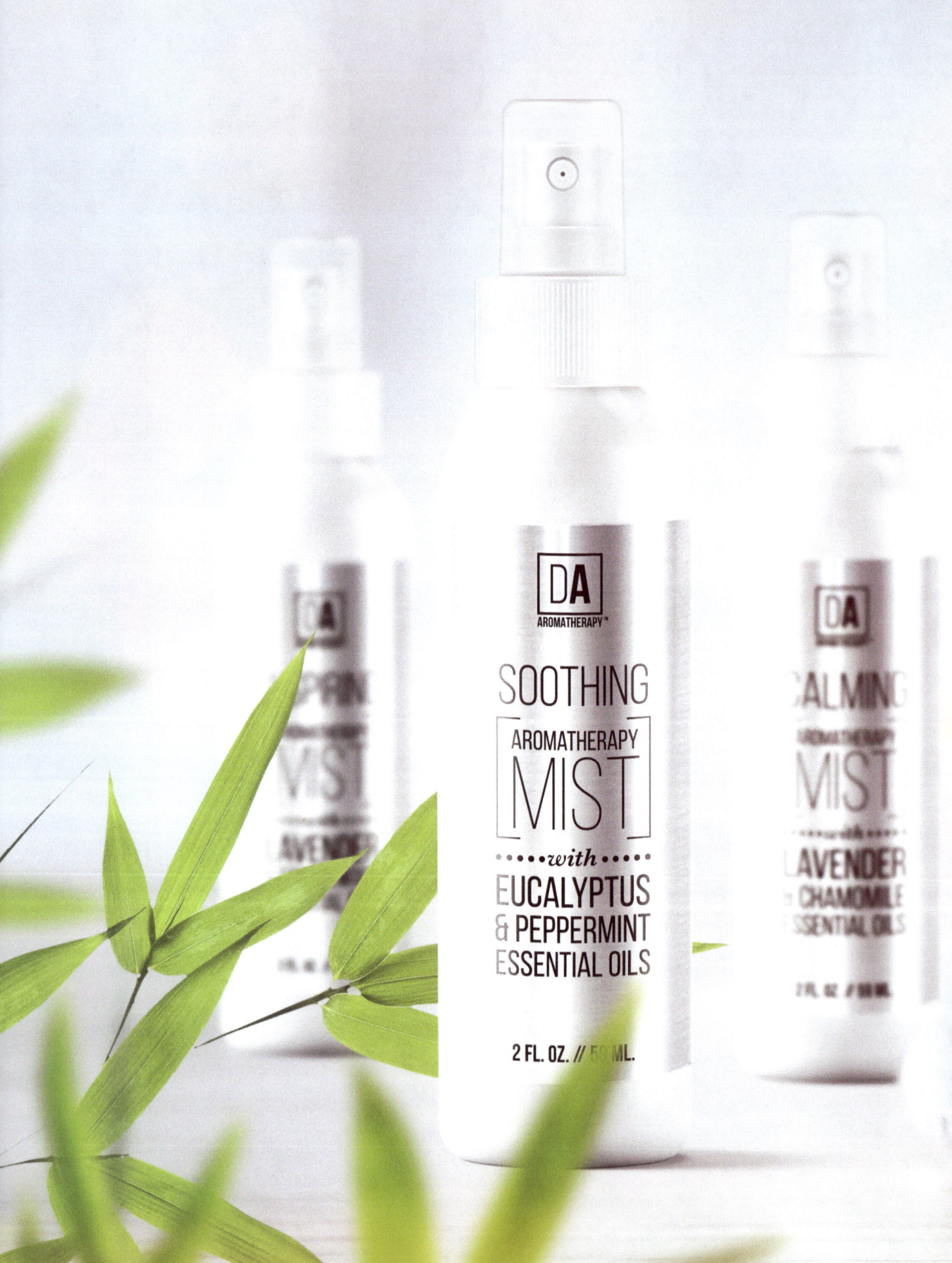

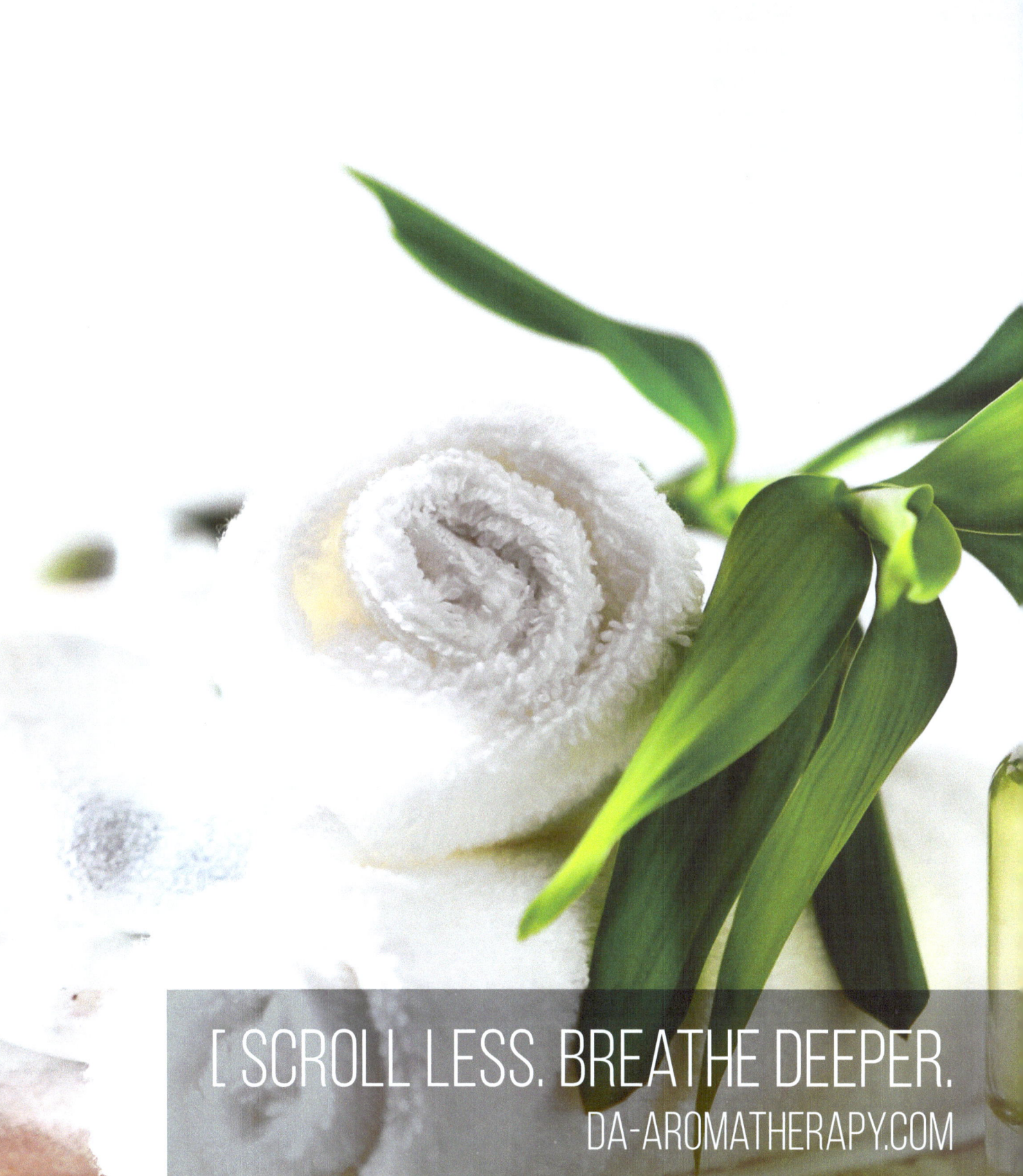

LUXURY REAL ESTATE
IN HUDSON VALLEY

ALEXANDER MAXWELL REALTY™

ALMAXREALTY.COM

info@almaxrealty.com
1-845-518-2750

www.ingramcontent.com/pod-product-compliance
Lightning Source LLC
Chambersburg PA
CBHW051223220526
45473CB00003B/1151